through her eyes

Life and Ministry of Women
in the Muslim World

through her eyes

Life and Ministry of Women in the Muslim World

Marti Smith

Authentic
MEDIA

Authentic Media
We welcome your comments and questions.
129 Mobilization Drive, Waynesboro, GA 30830 USA authenticusa@stl.org

and 9 Holdom Avenue, Bletchley, Milton Keynes, Bucks, MK1 1QR, UK
www.authenticbooks.com

If you would like a copy of our current catalog, contact us at:
1-8MORE-BOOKS
ordersusa@stl.org

Through Her Eyes
ISBN: 1-932805-07-9

Copyright © 2004 by Marti Smith

Library of Congress Cataloging-in-Publication Data

Smith, Marti, 1970-
 Through her eyes : life and ministry of women in the Muslim world / by Marti Smith.
   p. cm.
 ISBN 1-932805-07-9 (pbk.)
 1. Missions to Muslims. 2. Women missionaries. I. Title.

BV2625.S64 2005
266'.0088'297–dc22
                        2005002125

Cover design: Paul Lewis
Interior design: Angela Duerksen
Editorial team: Michaela Dodd, Betsy Weinrich, and Karen James

Printed in the United States of America

And this is my prayer: that your love may abound more and more in knowledge and depth of insight, so that you may be able to discern what is best and may be pure and blameless until the day of Christ, filled with the fruit of righteousness that comes through Jesus Christ—to the glory and praise of God.

Philippians 1:9-11

Contents

Part 3: Life under Pressure
Staying Anchored during Storms

Part 4: How Should We Live?
Questions of Culture, Values, and Money

Part 5: Singleness and Marriage
Living the Life God Gives You

Part 6: Parenting
Family Issues, Choices, and Models

Introduction

There aren't many people I admire as much as Vivian.* Her rare mix of stubborn perseverance, creativity, and compassion make her an excellent role model. But when I see and hear what she's been through as a pioneer missionary and mother of five, I sometimes find myself thinking, "I could never do that!"

After seven years as a mission mobilizer and trainer, I had the chance to get a closer look. I spent a year on the field with Vivian and the church-planting team she and her husband lead. I wanted to experience life as a rookie missionary and learn from experienced men and women. It seemed a good opportunity to put my skills as a researcher and writer to use, too: by doing interviews and writing articles I could help field missionaries tell their stories to equip and inspire others. "You should write about the women," Vivian insisted.

Today, well over half of the people who call themselves church planters are women, and many of those women are raising children at the same time. Most have even less time than their husbands to teach, write, and share their stories so that others may benefit from their experiences. Who will help other women see that what may seem impossible can indeed be done? These stories need to be told.

I knew the challenges of being a single woman in the Muslim world, but I quickly saw that the challenges faced by my friends who were young mothers were greater. Both the single women and the married women I met tended to have less of a support network than they needed. Yet their health, happiness, and effectiveness is an important part of seeing the gospel taken to the world's women.

---

* Like all the names used in this book, this is a pseudonym.

So, while living in Central Asia, I spent some of my time traveling from city to city interviewing missionary women, a process I continued after returning to the States. Listening to their stories, I was struck by how much of what they said has broader applications. These stories seem to deal with what it means to be a follower of Christ, what it means to be a woman, even what it means to be human.

So Many Challenges

Missionaries in a pioneer situation, where there has been no breakthrough for the gospel, usually lack the safety net that language schools, missionary visas, and tried-and-true methods of ministry provide. For many women in this situation, several questions persist: How do you learn a language, keep your job and visa, raise and teach your kids, reach out with the love of Christ, and explain what you are doing to the people around you? When you have young children around, can and should you do all those things? Are some approaches to these questions inherently better than others? What principles will help you balance your life and make decisions?

Anticipating these challenges keeps many women from even considering missions. "I could never do what you do," they say, as I did. Then, arriving on the field, many women find themselves saying, "Nobody told me it would be like this. How am I going to survive, much less have anything to contribute?"

This book is primarily written to aid, support, and encourage women like those it profiles: women living in mission settings among people who have little or no access to the church. I want to see them stay on the field—and prosper. In setting these experiences down on paper, I hope to encourage and equip more women, both married and single, to see that the obstacles they face in ministry can be surmounted. I want you to be able to say, as I could after spending a year with Vivian and her team, "Maybe I *can* picture myself doing that."

A Brief History

If God is calling you to be a missionary, you can know that you're not alone. You join a long line of faithful women who have faced and overcome many challenges and much ambiguity. In the early years of modern missions, women could only serve in mission agencies in the roles of wives and mothers. Very few single women were accepted as missionaries. After facing this discrimination, they ended up creating their own structures which were led, prayed for, and funded by women's missionary society groups in local churches. In turn, these groups would send out only women (that is to say, single women). By 1900 there were more than forty women's mission societies in the United States alone. By that year, the number of women in missions outnumbered men for the first time.

The ratio of women to men increased rapidly. Men had—and have—far more opportunities to serve in ministry and leadership in their home countries; this may be a factor. In one province of China in 1910, there were seventy-nine women and forty-six men among the Baptists and Presbyterians. The ratio of single women continued to climb until in many places women outnumbered men two-to-one.[1]

This means that today's mission force may be two-thirds female. I interviewed a woman who works in Turkey who said that of the one hundred people there with her mission agency, there are thirty-five married couples, twenty-five single women, and just five single men. Representatives of another agency also say they are seeing women respond to the call in great numbers. In 2002 women comprised 75 percent of their short-term team applicants.[2]

It seems that women may be more willing to go to the mission field than men are. And, in spite of the limitations they may face, many of the women God has raised up are very effective. When missionary Lottie Moon made significant inroads in evangelism, church planting, and training indigenous leaders, one of her supervisors exclaimed, "I estimate a single woman in China is worth two married men!"[3]

Telling Their Stories

Despite the increase in numbers, women in missions are confronted with the reality that serving cross-culturally is incredibly humbling. It's also a joy and a privilege. This book attempts to tell both sides of that story, revealing the situations and emotions frontier missionaries struggle with, particularly those that are common to wives and mothers. Not all their experiences, or the conclusions missionaries draw from them, are the same; they reflect a variety of situations, personalities, and responses. Each short chapter in this book focuses on the experiences of a particular woman and tells her story as she told it to me, through her eyes. These women are working in "closed" Muslim countries, and their identities must be protected. I am sorry I cannot share many details of each woman's life and ministry, nor use their real names.

This is not a how-to manual; it is a collection of stories, the stories of just two dozen women working in Central Asia and other parts of the Muslim world. Most are North American, Australian, British, or South African. Because the earliest interviews were conducted in 2002, some of these women's life situations have changed since their stories were written. Some of them may seem quite bleak. Many of the women interviewed seemed to be saving up the most emotional things they had experienced to share during interviews. They did so to give glory to God—to show others that in spite of our weakness and the many challenges we face, he is advancing his kingdom, in our lives and families and among those we serve. As you read, you will see that in spite of many obstacles, living a healthy life and having an effective ministry in a frontier mission field can be done—and that there's more than one way to do it. That may be the most important lesson I learned: to keep striving and looking for a better way to do things but relax in the knowledge that there may be many paths. You do not have to be just like someone else.

Discussion questions at the end of each section will help you evaluate what you are reading and discuss how to apply it in your own situation. If possible, I encourage you to read this book in community. Use it to help you articulate your own convictions and describe your own experiences.

Acknowledgments

Among the resources I found helpful in this project was the magazine *Women of the Harvest,* which is designed to support and encourage women in cross-cultural missions. *Women of the Harvest* also organizes retreats that bring together missionary women for fellowship and refreshment. Please contact Women of the Harvest for more information.

Women of the Harvest
PO Box 151297
Lakewood, CO 80215-9297 USA
Tel: 303.985.2148
www.womenoftheharvest.com
info@womenoftheharvest.com

For a more ministry-focused resource I turned to *Ministry to Muslim Women: Longing to Call Them Sisters*[4] and *From Fear to Faith: Muslim and Christian Women.*[5] Since I began work on this manuscript, many more books about understanding and reaching out to Muslims have been published or returned to print, including Christine Mallouhi's *Miniskirts, Mothers and Muslims: A Christian Woman in a Muslim Land,*[6] the first edition of which shaped many of my assumptions about ministry in the Muslim world.

During my year in Central Asia I interviewed several dozen women about their experiences, philosophies, hopes, fears, and lessons learned; those interviews were used to write the bulk of this book. For those women, that year, my team on the field, the support of my organization, Caleb Project, in this endeavor, and the skill of my editor, Michaela, I am exceedingly grateful.

—Marti Smith

Part 1:
Adjustment and Perseverance

Being Called, Equipped, and Made Effective

1 Pajamas in Perspective

Almost ten years ago we drove from the airport to the place we would stay for our first six weeks in this country. I sat looking out the window, soaking in all the impressions of the place where I expected to spend at least the next decade of my life.[*]

As newcomers, my husband and I wondered just how we should live. What should our home look like? How should we dress? In a cosmopolitan setting, several cultures and standards may exist side by side, so it wasn't easy. We chose to identify with the majority, the mainstream of our unreached group. Convicted by the fact that these people had never seen what a believer or a believing family in their culture might look like, we felt burdened to model godliness as much as we possibly could. That would mean becoming as much like them as possible. Our approach, however, was not without its costs. And I began to feel the cost pretty quickly—in the price of my identity.

Even on that first drive from the airport, I noticed that the women, especially those in the suburbs, wore brightly colored head-scarves and dresses with pants underneath. But their outfits never matched! Some also wore quilted robes to keep them warm around the neighborhood. They were the kind of robes we would use over pajamas back in the States. To my western eyes, these women looked so sloppy! "God," I prayed, "Am I going to have to wear 'pajamas' for the next ten years of my life?"

---

[*] By Vivian Rowland. Originally published in *Women of the Harvest*. For more about Vivian, see chapter 7. Why Moms Should Learn the Language, 15. Bringing the Gospel of Peace, 18. A Troubled Believer, 20. Jesus in the Hospital Ward, 23. Available in the Busiest Season, 42. Even a Healthy Marriage . . . , and 53. One-Room Schoolhouse.

The First Two Years

The two years that followed were challenging, to say the least. When we began I had a two-year-old and a two-month-old. Disposable diapers weren't available, and neither was anything I could recognize as a washing machine. Our main goals for these first few years were to learn the language and build relationships, but with my babies to take care of, how was I going to do either? We moved in with a local family to immerse ourselves in the language and culture. I am so glad; as a busy mom this was the only way I was going to get the contact I needed.

Who Am I?

About three weeks after moving in with the local family, I found myself spending one long morning squatting on the concrete floor of the bathroom washing thirty dirty diapers. I questioned again: Who was I becoming? Back in my home country my role had involved thinking, strategizing, analyzing, and planning. Who was I now? Who was I going to become in order to identify and relate with these women?

At that moment I didn't like the woman I pictured myself becoming. I wanted to go home! But God began ministering to my heart and mind. I realized I wanted to do what it would take to reach these people, no matter how uncomfortable and distasteful it might be.

Another morning, I was trying to study. My baby cried from his bed; once again my work was interrupted. Glancing out the window through my tears, I saw a neighbor woman, standing in nine inches of snow to pour warm water over her husband's head as he washed his hair. My neighbor also cooked out in the snow. She did her laundry out in the snow. Her little shack of a home was not very warm. In fact, her whole life consisted of working to keep her family clothed, warm, and fed.

Grace to Live like My Neighbors

Tears now streaming down my face, I saw my sufferings and complaints in perspective. I had been among the privileged 15 percent of women in the world who live with modern conveniences and comfort. In contrast, most of the world's women spend their lives in manual labor on behalf of their families. If those 85 percent could do it, by God's grace I could too.

God spoke to my heart and showed me he had not sent me to call these women to a more comfortable life; he had sent me to demonstrate a joyful and abundant life in the midst of circumstances like theirs. That meant I was to move toward them just as Christ moved toward us. After all, hadn't Jesus emptied himself and had become man in the ultimate identity sacrifice?

Adjustment never feels good. God showed me I didn't need to worry about who I was becoming or what my identity was. I just needed to live for him: to keep plugging away in life and in language learning with joy and contentment. If I was willing to draw close to these women, yes, my identity would change, but it would all be worth it.

Two Years Later

Two years later I found myself sitting in my living room, laughing with a dear local friend as she told me a joke. I thought about the scarf and "pajamas" I now wore most days of my life, and realized that my identity was more "housewife" than it had ever been before. The amazing part was, I didn't mind!

For two years I had pushed to put language learning and relationship building first. Peeling off my western-ness and putting on the local ways had been a hard adjustment. I still felt limited in my language and tongue-tied when I tried to share with my friends on an emotional level. But I had local friends who came to see me, laughed with me, trusted me with secrets, and even woke me at 2 a.m. in a crisis. I hoped with all my heart that some day they would share their spiritual hunger with me, and that I would be able to share the love of God with them.

A Fruitful Ministry

Today, many years later, it's happening and has been for some time. I still get tongue-tied at times but, thanks to God, I'm able to share the Good News and discuss spiritual things with my friends. My days are filling up with "ministry." Sometimes I had wondered if those days would ever come. It's God's timing. He's bringing openhearted women into my path. I just happen to be available and have a little language and cultural bonding under my belt.

God will never take something from us without giving us something better. I lost one identity but gained another. As we release our lives, identities, and habits, we can put them into the trustworthy hands of the one who gave all he had for us. He offers us fulfillment and life we can never lose. Challenges come, and I still hear myself complain, but I quickly remind myself how truly glad I am to be where I am and doing what I'm doing. I wouldn't trade my life for anything!

2 Cultural Immersion

Until a few years ago Isabelle,[*] a single woman, had not spent much time overseas, and even less in a ministry context. Then four years ago, she moved to Central Asia to join a church-planting team. At the beginning, she did not know what to expect. "I knew I'd be teaching the team's five school-aged kids. And I knew I'd be immersed in the country's language and culture."

From the beginning, Isabelle's team was committed to helping her adjust to cross-cultural living. She wanted to learn the language, culture, and ways of the Central Asian people she lived among, and living with a local family was the best way to do it. "So on my second day in town, I moved out to a village on the outskirts of the city. Our house had no phone to connect to the city, and no running water. There was an outhouse that was just a hole in the dirt floor, and I had to take bucket baths. That wasn't such a big deal, but the fact that they were Muslims and did not speak any English was." She came into the city regularly, but she lived in the village. She would have to learn to adapt.

Living with a Local Family

Isabelle's team knew quite well the family she would be living with. They knew this family would take good care of her, and they did. They even gave Isabelle her own room, humoring a Western preference they must have found strange. Wouldn't she be lonely? Actually, says Isabelle, living with the family felt quite confining at first.

"I'd been an introverted girl living on my own, and now I was in a community-minded family that seemed to think things like,

---

[*] For more about Isabelle, see chapter 11. Looking Forward to Going Back, 41. Who Will Listen to a Single Woman? and 53. One-Room Schoolhouse.

'Why *wouldn't* the brothers go through your stuff and steal your deodorant?' I was being dragged to parties all the time, and my 'mom,' Olivia, was always watching over me and trying to protect me. I'd catch her looking at me all the time. Don't get me wrong, they were a great family; it was just a matter of me adjusting."

If Isabelle got sick, the family tried all the remedies they knew, some of which seemed bizarre to a woman used to Western medicine. "They said, 'Eat, eat!' all the time, making sure I was fat enough. It was really hard at first!"

In time Isabelle came to realize she wasn't the only one making sacrifices. After all, this family had taken her into their home and patiently tried to communicate with her and understand her ways. "I realized *they* were the ones who took in this incompetent American girl. They were so patient with my crying fits. They got used to me! 'Oh Isabelle, she just cries.'"

Back in America Isabelle's own parents were somewhat wrapped up in their own problems. They were going through a divorce, did not write to her much, and never called. "So I felt like I didn't have a family, and here was this family that took me in as their own. We were connected."

A New Identity

During these and other adjustments that came in her first year, Isabelle broke down in tears quite often. She was just getting to know her teammates, and they all seemed miles ahead of her. She did not see how she could make a contribution. Due to her team's urgent need for someone to teach their children and their healthy financial situation, Isabelle had been spared the long period of raising support that comes between most people's decision to go to the field and actual arrival overseas. She had come after only a few months. And to get there she had given up, among other things, her professional career. "My whole identity changed. I had been an economist before, and now what? I felt like everything that defined who I was at that time was suddenly gone. I had to get in touch with all these new sides of me which I didn't know if I liked."

Although she is usually fairly flexible and amenable, Isabelle

Adjustment and Perserverance

found herself chafing against the restrictions she had to follow to avoid raising eyebrows in her traditional community. The only other singles on her team were men, and she could only visit them with chaperones, such as one of the families on the team. She played volleyball with the guys at times and enjoyed the easy conversation and relaxed environment, but some teammates started to wonder if even that was appropriate. The families took her in when they could, but they could not meet all of her relational needs and take care of her all the time. And whenever she was out, she had to try to get home before sundown.

"I felt like I needed more interaction for encouragement, to keep going, and I couldn't find it. It was hard to find it with Central Asians because I didn't have enough language, and besides I needed to be this different person with them, a person I wasn't comfortable with yet. I didn't know what to do. 'Well, you could die to yourself,' God said to me. It sounds harsh, but it was true. I felt like I had a need and was going to have to let it die, and trust God. Obviously God didn't think I 'needed' it or he'd have made a way. So I learned that if I don't have something I think I need, I have to trust that I'm going to be okay."

It was after that point that Isabelle began to like the Central Asian sides of her personality that were now emerging. "It's like God has expanded my identity to include this whole other part of me I didn't know about, a part that likes glittery lipsticks and funny sandals and big hair! I just enjoy it! And all the dancing and everything; people just don't get to dance like this in the States! At first those things were burdens, but they became part of my whole identity. I learned to love my assertive Central Asian side. Bargaining is so much fun; I love all the drama associated with it. You play it cool, pretend you don't like the item, and walk off to get the price down—then bring up some excuse to come back because you have to get it after all for your uncle or something. Even dealing with boys who flirt with you and learning how to shame them by saying things like 'Don't you have a mother?' It's all fun for me now." Probably the most helpful thing is that she now speaks the local language comfortably. She is not much of an outsider anymore.

❀ Cultural Immersion

Continuing the Relationship with Her Local Family

After living with her Central Asian family for a year, Isabelle felt it was time to move into the city. However, she returns to the village almost every week for a visit. These visits are a joy to both her and the family. "I know when I walk into the kitchen, Olivia will be making some delicious food because she always tries to make my favorite dishes when I come. That's the heart of a true mother, a mother to the Central Asian side of me especially! I know she's always going to look forward to me coming, and I'll look forward to seeing her. They are my family: my brothers and my mother and my sister-in-law. They are not a project. I can kick back and watch TV or joke around. I'm part of the 'in circle' with them, all language barriers aside. I know I'm a part of that family, and it's really a blessing. If I ever do leave Central Asia it will be really hard, knowing these people who are such a big part of my life are on the other side of the world."

How much Isabelle had come to care about her Central Asian family really hit home after Olivia became a believer in Christ. "I realize I will see her in heaven. We're going to be together up there for eternity. It brought a whole new meaning to evangelism. These are not just faceless people, but people who have taken me in. It makes me really want to see the rest of the family come to Christ."

Benefits of Immersion

After four years, the things Isabelle has learned from the local culture have made her more capable and competent in dealing with practical challenges as they come along. "This year I woke up at 4:00 one morning to find it was raining from my ceiling! A pipe had broken in the apartment above, and nobody was there. It was raining, not only in my bathroom, but in the bedroom as well. I went and knocked on the neighbor's door and got a number to call. I was so excited: I had to rely entirely on the local system and was able to communicate my needs over the phone; I never had to call a teammate. I can communicate, get along, and participate in relationships and community life on my own."

Is it worth the emotional pain of immersion to get to that point? The pain of never becoming capable in a society would be much worse, Isabelle believes, but the route she chose was also difficult. "Immersion is going to sap you. Everything is unfamiliar. You have to let go of a lot of yourself, and that's going to wear you out." At first there is a huge learning curve. You are becoming part of a team, wearing and eating new things and learning a language you knew nothing about before. "Every single area of my life was different. On the other hand, I cannot imagine *not* doing it. You reap benefits as time goes on. Immersion is not sapping me now. It's energizing me and giving me the coping skills to do it well and even thrive here. It's become much more natural.

"When I go back to America, I think I'm going to be uncomfortable. But since I spend most of the year here, I think it's worth it. I'm naturally more Central Asian now. I didn't realize how much until I went to Thailand for vacation. I'd been feeling like a foreigner here, but when I went there I saw how Central Asian I'd become and how much I'd adapted Central Asian ways of looking at things."

Isabelle knows she has not arrived; there are still days when she feels very much the outsider, and it may always be that way. Yet she has learned to like the new, bi-cultural person she has become. "You think immersion gets you wet on the outside and you can get out and dry off, but it's more like ink than water. It soaks into you and becomes part of who you are."

3　Loneliness and Adjustment

Connie* began her ministry in the Muslim world more than a dozen years ago. She and her husband helped pioneer new work in a Muslim country in South Asia. Now in Central Asia, she is grateful for the experiences she had and lessons she learned in her first ministry field—experiences and lessons she now passes on to women who are just getting started in situations like hers.

At this point, Connie's children are grown, but when they were small, she had few role models. Church planting in the Muslim world was beginning to experience a resurgence, but with the new efforts came an old prejudice. It was a time when many missionaries and church planters did not think they had much to learn from those who preceded them. "If the gospel was to go where it had not gone before, missionaries had to break the mold," explains Connie. Besides, none of the other Christian workers she knew were on the field with their school-age children. Who could understand her situation and give her good advice? There seemed to be nobody. Those circumstances only heightened the effects of what is probably a universal human problem—loneliness.

Naming Fears and Soliciting Prayer

Connie and her husband were reaching out to a specific population within the refugee community in their host country—a minority within a minority. The challenges were great. "We knew we couldn't live among them right away, so we'd have to live somewhere else and just see how to get in." Connie's

---

* For more about Connie, see chapter 33. Choosing Where to Live and 52. The Right School for Your Kids.

expectations were quite simple: "I expected to learn language, build relationships with Muslims, and investigate ways to reach the people we were interested in."

However, to reach people like that, she would need to leave behind the world she had known. "Loneliness was my biggest concern and my biggest fear," says Connie. Whatever she was most afraid of, she believed, would be her area of greatest vulnerability. So Connie and her husband both felt they needed to name their fears and turn them into prayer requests.

"I asked people at home to pray for another foreigner to be my friend, for a national Christian friend, and for a friend in the unreached community we were focusing on." Then she sat back and watched God answer her prayers.

"Well, my fear was accurate," she admits. "I was very lonely. I knew the facts of the situation when I was going into it, but I didn't really know the magnitude of the loneliness. Nobody prepared me for that. No one could! It's the kind of thing that has to be experienced. We went in not knowing a soul and not knowing who could help us. The only two people we knew in the whole country were two single guys with our organization."

Answers to Prayer

Early on, one of the single men on their team was able to introduce Connie and her husband to a local Christian family who had kids. It wasn't quite the same as having a friend from her home culture, but the wife took Connie around to get clothes and taught her how to dress and behave, and their kids kept each other entertained. "They would play camping together and builds tents in the living room," says Connie. Soon Connie and her husband found other Christian friends, both foreigners and locals, and became part of an international church.

Making friends in the broader community was more challenging. In the society Connie lived in, most significant relationships are within the family. It was almost impossible for an outsider to get in. Connie's next-door neighbors were also her landlords, though, and the wife became one of her first friends. But as a member of the city's upper-class Muslim community, this woman never left her house. "We were actually in the same 'compound,' but she only came to visit me twice; I always had to go to her."

Making friends in the refugee community they were interested in serving was another challenge. For one thing, the refugees did not speak the trade language Connie was trying to learn first. She only knew a few words of their "heart language," the language they spoke at home and preferred. Connie remembers the first day she and her husband went to check things out. "I was totally lost and overwhelmed. We were very focused, though. We knew what we needed to do and were willing to do whatever it took. You have to be an over-comer for the sake of your goal.

"We met a refugee woman that day. It was like the Lord had given us a supernatural understanding and knit our hearts together when our eyes met. 'Come to my house,' she said. You have to seize these moments! We went to her tent in the camp and had tea together. We went to visit her many times after that, whenever we went out to the camp, and I even took my mother to meet her when she came.

"We moved to a new city the next year and only saw this woman twice after that. The point is, even if that person isn't going to be your best friend all the time, you need someone in the beginning. We women, especially, need that motivation," says Connie. "This relationship gave me a reason to care, a reason to try."

Learning the Language

Besides these initial friendships, Connie knew the best thing she could invest in to equip her for ministry and contentment in her host culture was learning the language, or languages. But she got off to a rocky start. "We had studied the LAMP* method and did it for maybe two or three months without much success."

In the conservative Muslim community where Connie was

* Language Acquisition Made Practical is a method for learning languages while building relationships. It was developed by Thomas and Elizabeth Brewster.

living, local women stayed behind high walls and closed doors. "Relational" language-learning methods had to overcome these challenges. In her vulnerability, Connie blamed not the circumstances or the methods, but herself. "'I'm a failure!' I thought. 'This is horrible!'"

"We had stayed in touch with the woman who had taught our LAMP class, so I wrote to her, saying how discouraged I was and how it wasn't working. She made a special trip to our city to see us. She was there less than thirty-six hours, but she came! It was such a big help. She helped us find ways to use the principles and adapt them to fit our situation."

A visit from a sympathetic coach can work wonders when you are discouraged, and help you see how to try things a little differently rather than throwing out the tools that did not seem to work.

In her language study, as well as in overcoming loneliness, building relationships, and beginning a ministry, Connie learned an important truth: her reality might not measure up to her ideals. "You have to learn to merge your idealism with your reality! It's good to be idealistic, but what motivates us also creates high expectations within us, expectations for ourselves. Then we feel our failure very keenly," says Connie. "I've seen this with women all over the world."

4 Are We Staying or Going?

Angela* and her husband, David, have been in Central Asia for four years and are just now preparing for their first furlough. Over the years, there were times when they wondered if their family would make it, but now they can't believe they made it four years. Although they have traveled a long journey since arriving on the field, just getting to the field was a long journey in and of itself.

One key step along the way was the year they spent in East Africa shortly after David finished his studies in veterinary medicine. "It was an old-fashioned mission compound, big trucks and everything; David filled a veterinary position, and I worked in the office. We saw it as something to do after college before we started 'real life.' A lot of retired folks came to work for a year or two. We thought, 'That's what we'll do—come back when we are retired,'" says Angela with a laugh. "Meanwhile we'll have our 2.5 kids and our careers . . . after we're rich, we'll come back!"

The work in Africa was a good experience, but Angela and her husband were young in their faith and marriage and not ready for something more demanding, she says. They returned home to the States and did not think much about moving overseas again. However, God was orchestrating events in their lives to equip them. "He took the next ten years to train us! Our church and other responsibilities helped to make us ready.

"When you figure one thing out, God gives you something a little bigger. During that time one of us would say, 'Maybe God wants us to go . . .', and the other would say, 'No way!' There was always a reason: David had just started a new clinic, and I had

---

* For more about Angela, see chapter 36. The Comparison Trap.

Adjustment and Perserverance

these babies. . . . Finally, in the eighth year God said to both of us, 'Now it's time.'"

Even so, Angela says, they "sat on it" for a whole year. "We wanted to make sure it wasn't just a mid-life thing," she explains. In the year before they made the decision public, David and Angela talked to their pastor and his wife and asked the deacons of the church to pray for them. Their mission agency required David to complete twenty hours of seminary, which required the couple to relocate for a season. "That wasn't so bad: it was close to both our families; we had grandmas an hour away! We finished seminary, and then we came to Central Asia."

Adjusting to the Field

In some ways Central Asia was a big step for David and Angela, although their previous experience in East Africa gave them some understanding of what life in a third-world country was like. But there were some big differences: during their first exposure to life as missionaries, they had been a young married couple; now they were a family with four kids. Fortunately, some aspects of their experience were easier. Previous workers had already remodeled the house in which they were living; they joined an existing team, and David had four or five months for language learning before he began work.

"Coming back to the field with kids was a totally new ballgame!" says Angela. "Our first year was hard; our first two and a half or three years were hard. In fact, in the first year, if I'd had enough language and knew where the airline ticket office was, I would have left!"

Although things were not particularly difficult for the kids, going to the field as a mother meant Angela had a more complicated life than she had experienced in Africa. That seemed to magnify the various stresses of the transition. Like many other women who have lived overseas as single or childless women before they became mothers, she was surprised at how different her experience was.

"We arrived the day after Christmas. Because we'd been training and preparing all that fall, we had not been 'doing school.'

My oldest, at seven, was already behind in reading and writing. My biggest 'heartache' was that I knew they needed to start school again." Anxious for her children, Angela decided to make homeschooling her first priority. She wonders now if that was wise. "You can tell someone that shouldn't be the only priority, looking back, but how much can she quite get it? I gave myself just a month to get settled in, and we started homeschooling in February. I never had time to adjust." And she never had time for learning the local language.

The First Few Years

Before they came to the field, several people gave David and Angela some sound advice that she has found very helpful. "One couple, who had been in South America for ten years or so, told us, 'Your relationships with locals are what will make a difference in whether your ministry is effective, but your relationships with your team are what will make a difference in whether you stay.'"

Angela thought she needed more team support than she was getting, although looking back she understands the other pressures teammates were under at that time. "God used all that to help me grow, but it made the first year harder. Several times I thought we would leave the country. At least once David said, 'You have got to decide, are we staying or going? We need to talk about it and decide; we can't go on like this!'

"The other advice we got came from an elderly pastor, who said, 'Never doubt in the dark what you knew to be true in the light.' That helped me in those first years. Even though I was in the dark, I knew he had called us to come. That helped me to not grab hold of how I felt at the moment."

Angela came to the conclusion that if God had called them and had not told them to go home, they were supposed to stay. "It didn't help my attitude, but it meant going home wasn't an option! Once that was dealt with, things have gotten better."

Too Tired to Talk

The last few years have been hard on David and Angela's relationship with one another. "In the States we had a very secure marriage, and others held us up as a good example. I was almost to the point of being prideful about that. But the first couple of years we were here, we quit talking! He would get up and leave in the mornings, then come back and go to bed, or conk out in front of the TV set. He didn't want to think.

"The first couple years at least, you are just too tired. Nobody wants to talk, certainly about anything serious. For a good amount of the day, we're not connected, but we both need to share that with someone. I need him to encourage me and help me deal with issues that may come up."

In order to strengthen their relationship with each other, David and Angela made a plan to go out for lunch once a week. Their destinations are not exciting: "Either we go to the one place that's not too bad or the other one!" says Angela. Their house helper stays with their kids. "We may have a 'How is life?' discussion, or we may not talk about anything at all, but we are alone together, and not exhausted like we sometimes are at night. We've tried to schedule it every week. It's important just to keep conversation going. I try to take an interest in what he's doing with work and ministry, and he takes time to ask about the kids and school, so we stay in touch."

Taking Breaks

In their first year, especially, they needed frequent breaks, but getting out of the city they were living in seemed more stressful than staying put. Most of the people in the large, nearby city speak a different local language than the one Angela and her family are studying. But in time, they discovered getting away was too important to skip, even if it had stresses of its own. Once they learned their way around the big city, they found visits there could be relaxing. Similarly, getting out of the country entirely from time to time is worth the effort.

"We take a three-week vacation once a year, usually in Thailand. It's nice to get away and be the tourist. I can't imagine, reading William Carey, what it would be like to go for six years with no vacations!"

Like many families with multiple children, Angela looks at

her upcoming furlough with mixed emotions. Packing, moving, and traveling are not easy with four children. "We are trying to keep things simple. We are from the same hometown, and our folks are still living there. We have some churches to speak in, and we have to go to headquarters. But for most of the time, we will park my dad's trailer at the lake and have people come to us. It will be nice to let our kids have the freedom to run around. We don't feel we can do that here, because none of them have picked up the language well enough."

Seeing the Way Ahead

Nothing has changed on the outside, but after several years of wondering if they were staying or going, something changed in their perspective. Angela is excited to take on some new challenges. "David has got us hooked up to propane for the winter, and he knows how to work with electricity. I'd just as soon not have a lot of stuff; I don't need much. So we're planning to move out of the city."

Her husband is seeing fruit in his ministry relationships, to the extent that nearly all the men he works with have become believers. He's instilled in them a vision to use their humanitarian work for evangelism. "We'd like to take the work to a smaller town and use it as a hub to move out into villages," explains Angela, the excitement in her voice growing. "When we come back from furlough, that's where we'd like to be, making exploratory trips." Far from wondering if she and her family can make it on the field, she now has a vision to mobilize and minister to others. "We are really praying for a team of local believers to go with us!"

5 Those Who Persevere

Things seem to keep changing. Wars, unrest, the departure of teammates, and health problems make the situation in Ginny's South Asian host country uncertain. For the last few years her family has not been in one place for more than six months at a time. Learning the local language, making friends, putting down roots, and finding her place in effective ministry still seem like elusive goals. When all but one of the other Christian families with young children left her city, Ginny* was discouraged about what it would mean for her two young sons.

"Week after week, our three-year-old son, Liam, was saying goodbye to more of his little friends, maybe forever. There was only one other family left. We decided that if the last family left, it would be something we should consider as well."

Today, Ginny's family is also off the field, for now. When the government refused to renew their visas, it was a confirmation of what they already suspected, that they would need to spend a longer season out of the country. It was something of a relief; they need renewal. But all of these changes have altered Ginny's attitudes, helped her see what she needs to "make it" in ministry, and taught her how to give others a realistic view of long-term life on the field.

God's Commitment to You

"I used to get mad at the church and Christians in general, saying, 'Why aren't there more people willing to go to the tough places?' If you look at these big churches, and Christianity in general, it still irks me that more don't go. But the fact is that not everyone is made to make it in the very stressful places. That

* For more about Ginny, see chapter 25. Commitment under Crisis and 31. Life in Seclusion.

doesn't mean there is something wrong with them, and it doesn't mean those who do go are better people, either! I've seen that this kind of work is not something everyone can do, and it's not something we should judge people about. You may think you have the answers, but in a place like this where they are tested, you could fall apart. You could even fall away from the faith, feeling overwhelmed with doubts and questions. I think of C. S. Lewis, who had all these answers about the problem of suffering. Then his wife died, and his answers were nothing to him.

"If you fall apart, or something else breaks you or makes you go home, you know what? God is merciful. You aren't out of it forever. You fall down; he picks you back up again. You are still God's favorite!"

Eyes Open

What kind of people would Ginny like to see coming to the field where she works? To start with, they need to be able to persevere. "It boils down to how committed they are," she says. "Are they just committed to coming, and when real suffering comes, will they say, 'I'm out of here'? Is there depth to it? It helps if people have a somewhat 'real' picture of what it's like—and to a good degree you can have it. Most people come short-term before they commit long-term.

"When you come for a visit, have your eyes open. Look for what might not be great about coming back long-term. Then, be honest about it. You want to come with a vision and excitement, but if you just focus on the good, you may end up making lofty plans about what your life will be like. People who have a somewhat realistic picture of what it's like when they come seem to do much better that those who just come to change the world!

"Oh, that sounds bad, doesn't it?" Ginny says with a bit of a laugh. Yes, she wants to see people with a vision to change the world make it to the field. "But it may take a lifetime, and you may not be here to see it. So those who aren't honest about that don't last."

Reality Check

Ginny has seen this in her own life. She has had to put her expectations for herself and her ministry dreams on hold. Now, she says, "My primary commitment is to raise a healthy family. That, and to continue language learning. I do have a concern for orphan kids, and making sure some of the ladies I know get to go to the doctor. These women are at the bottom of the totem pole. What their in-laws, husbands, and sons need always comes first. Maybe I can have a ministry with them."

Understanding and accepting herself as God's beloved helps Ginny fight off the spirit of comparison and guilt over a lack of accomplishment, which plagues many missionary women. "With two kids, I am quite busy. It's quite fun most of the time. Before, yes, I used to feel guilty that I should do more ministry," she admits, then smiles. "Now I'm thinking, 'Nah!'

"It may take me ten years to get where I expected to be in three years," says Ginny. "But if we are there thirty years, it doesn't really matter. It is a frustrating thing, wanting to be where you aren't. I have seen other mothers struggle with that. So I don't feel so bad, like I'm not capable.

"Yes, we are in this for the long term. But if I never make it back to the field, I may be tempted to think, 'Oh my gosh, I failed.' God is greater than that. God is an awesome God; he has restored me again and again."

6 Marrying In

After five years of ministry in Central Asia as a single man, Daniel returned to his home in Australia to marry Laura.* They spent about a year together in their home country, then returned to the field together. Generally, their team's culture and policies try to protect newcomers and help them get up to speed by encouraging or requiring them to live with local families and to spend significant time focused only on learning the local language. Marrying into the ministry put Laura in a different situation, however. Her husband already had a broad network of friendships. Laura would be part of the ministry from the beginning. She would have to jump in, sink or swim. While Laura enjoyed the challenge of figuring out "who was who," winning their respect was a bit more difficult.

"We came in December, and by February they were having one of the discipleship seminars the team used to do at our house. One of the women reminisces about it with me now, years later, 'You cook such great food now!' she says, 'But do you remember, when we all came to your house and you'd only just come? The potatoes weren't cooked properly! We just ate them anyway, because we didn't want to embarrass you!'"

While Laura is grateful for the tolerance and forbearance of her local friends, it can rankle. And coming to the field five years behind her husband introduced a lot of inequality into their marriage, when what she and her husband both wanted was a partnership. "I've been here almost three years. Only last year I started contributing to the believers' discussions for the first time. They looked at me like, 'Oh, she's talking!' They were used to

* For more about Laura, see chapter 38. Hiring a House Helper and 43. Allowing Your Marriage to Change.

seeing me as Daniel's 'bride' who doesn't speak very well. I felt very awkward, and didn't feel like I had much respect among the people. They were happy for me to be here, and they liked me, but I was mostly Daniel's bride.

"We both hoped for doing ministry together, and we are trying to work together more, though in reality 'working together' looks like doing quite different things: to me it feels like I'm facilitating Daniel's ministry. I came to be a partner, and have ended up playing a support role."

Feeling Left Behind

"Another challenge for Daniel was figuring out how to help me. If I did not understand something or found something difficult in a relationship with a local person or the team, I'd have this expectation: 'I'm going to talk to my husband and he's going to be on my side!' He should say, 'Oh, I'm so sorry, have a good cry on my shoulder; do you feel better now?' and maybe offer a few pointers in the end!

"What I had to accept was that it was not just me on the line, but his ministry too. It was important to him that I 'made it' here, that I adjusted and understood things. So instead of comforting me, he would put on his 'orientation' hat. He'd say, 'Can't you see it's like that for this reason?' I felt unsupported. But the worst thing was it felt like it was 'us' versus 'them,' and I was the only 'them!' I'd think, 'You're supposed to be the person closest to me, and you're defending 'them!'

"I imagine that it's a lot easier to bond with your team members when you're all in the same boat, starting together. Culture shock tends to bring out the worst in people, but then at least you'd all be in it together. Constantly feeling like the only person who was dysfunctional on a team of highly 'together' people was really hard. I remember feeling like I just didn't have anything to contribute. Whenever I came up with a new idea someone was sure to say, 'Yep, we tried that. It didn't work.'

"In retrospect, I can see how hard it was on Daniel. Here I was, the person he loved most, struggling more than he'd ever seen me struggle before. He naturally wanted to help, and it must have been awful when I rejected his help, whatever the reason."

Ready-Made Friendships

There are good and bad aspects of marrying someone who already has an established ministry, says Laura. "When most people I know come into the country, their initial relationships are with their host family, language teachers, neighbors, and colleagues at work. My initial relationships were with my language helpers and the wives of Daniel's friends. You can only take on so many new relationships, and then your 'dance card' is full. My dance card got full pretty quickly with Daniel's friends.

"Since Daniel had been here five years, most of his friends were believers. My language teachers were Muslims, but not very typical ones; they were all highly intelligent, educated, modern young women. I just did not have the emotional energy to pursue relationships with neighbors, who were more typical Muslims. Intellectually, I know this is okay. In fact, it probably fits who I am and my gifts well. But I still feel guilty about it; I was not spending much time 'in the culture.' It would have helped to have someone say, 'Hey, you're doing well.'"

Moving toward Partnership

Laura has had almost three years to catch up. While her husband still speaks the language more fluently than she does, she is now able to make a contribution both to team life and the church-planting ministry. Now, she realizes, she has paid her dues and been through most of what she calls the "hard stuff." She and Daniel are even partners in ministry to some extent. However, the expectations of the conservative culture in which they are working and the recent addition of a baby to their family limit Laura's ability to do what she thinks of as ministry.

"We did a Bible study on marriage with Victor and Sharon, two of the local believers. We were doing it together, kind of. Daniel would prepare the study. I'd ask him what was going on and have him explain a few words I didn't know. Then I'd prepare the meal and be dealing with that, and with Sharon's baby who was usually tearing up our house. Daniel would teach the lesson, and I would participate in the discussion. Back in Australia we would preach together. So it's a very different level of partnership."

While coming to the field five years behind her husband is difficult, Laura suspects it would be even harder for a man to join his wife's ministry field and struggle to catch up. A good friend of hers is in that very situation though, and seems to be doing well. "Carrie is a great encourager. I'm sure that's helped," says Laura. "So has the fact that they came back to the field with a six-month-old baby in tow." This makes Carrie and her husband more equal than they would be otherwise: both are going through adjustments. Her husband has had to take up the reins of the ministry while Carrie takes care of the baby. Carrie and her husband, like Laura and Daniel, are moving into a different kind of partnership.

7 Why Moms Should Learn the Language

"Why are things so much easier for men?" Vivian* asks. Many moms on the field ask that question and sigh, and one of the biggest areas they think of is language study. Even women who are brilliant language learners may find themselves lagging behind their husbands simply because they don't have the time for study or lessons while they manage kids, cooking, laundry, visitors, and other aspects of daily life overseas—tasks that fall more often on the wife than the husband. Vivian's husband, Trent, knew, however, that that both of them need to be able to minister in the local language in order to see their church-planting ministry—and their family—prosper. As a result, he made sure to value Vivian's language learning as much as his own.

Ways to Help

From the beginning Trent believed that encouraging Vivian to learn the language was an important investment, not just something that would be nice. "Many men don't come in thinking that," says Vivian. "Many women don't either." A husband who values his wife's language learning can find ways to help her through it.

One way Trent could facilitate Vivian's progress in learning the language was watching the kids. "On the days when I was focusing on the language, including both lessons and going to the bazaar or whatever, the kids were Trent's responsibility—for the whole day. I'd usually have a lesson in the morning and go see people in the afternoon. There were seasons when I had to

* For more about Vivian, see chapter 1. Pajamas in Perspective, 15. Bringing the Gospel of Peace, 18. A Troubled Believer, 20. Jesus in the Hospital Ward, 23. Available in the Busiest Season, 42. Even a Healthy Marriage . . . , and 53. One-Room Schoolhouse.

come home to nurse a baby, but it worked pretty well." Vivian recognizes that many men would find themselves in situations where they could not spend that much time at home, but her husband was studying at a university and arranged his schedule to allow it.

While taking formal lessons at the university was not a viable option for Vivian, she saw advantages in her own approach. Sometimes it was more work, but it was also more flexible. Vivian was able to set the pace of her own learning, find new language teachers when the ones she had were not the best, write her own lessons, and pick up more everyday language than her husband did.

Trent, on the other hand, memorized pages and pages of poetry written in a high literary style and tried to persevere through teaching techniques that were not very conducive to learning. However, he did learn things that Vivian did not. After class he would come home and pass on what he learned to her. She, in turn, worked to help and encourage him.

The two of them, along with other members of the team, used monthly evaluations of their language progress to track goals and language-learning approaches, as well as share what they were actually learning. Even now, after much of the team has been on the field for many years, they regularly set aside time to review their progress and encourage one another.[1]

Necessary for Ministry and Longevity

With so many demands on their attention, many women wonder if they really need to work on learning the local language. Indeed, for some ministries, language learning is not as critical. However, Vivian and Trent are called to a ministry of front-line discipleship and church planting that touches both men and women, and in a Muslim context, that may mean having largely separate, parallel ministries. "It wasn't that Trent was going to learn language and I would stay home and wash diapers," says Vivian. Trent could not disciple women; she would need to do that. And to do it well, she needed to speak the local language fluently.

Learning the language was not only key for her ministry, Vivian found, but also for her family. Having grown up an MK (missionary kid) and knowing many others, Vivian was concerned that she and her husband find healthy ways to raise well-adjusted children. She was surprised to learn how much learning the language could play a part in that. Without working hard to identify with the local people and speak their language, Vivian knew she would have a hard time feeling at home in her adopted culture. As she and her kids have identified with the local culture, learned the language, and learned to enjoy local ways, their level of stress has been reduced. Her kids are well adjusted and like living in their host country. They are happy to run errands and even show guests around the city without their parents' help. While they enjoy visits to their home country, they are also happy to return to Central Asia.

When the family took their first vacation in another country, Trent and Vivian stayed in a guesthouse run by a couple with five older kids. "Their kids were just the sweetest, healthiest kids, so I got together with the wife to see what I could learn from her," Vivian explains.

"Probably the biggest thing was this: in their sending agency, every wife must learn the language. The reason they have made that a rule is because they see that if the mother doesn't learn the language, she feels isolated, lonely, and unhappy with living in the country. How the mother feels makes the biggest difference with how the kids will feel. If you want to keep a family on the field—and happy—the mother must learn the language."

Another friend reinforced this message when she told Vivian, "If the woman doesn't learn the language, you can just count down the days until they leave!" The first few years were certainly challenging for Vivian, and her progress seemed slow at times. Now, however, because she can function well in the local culture and language, Vivian enjoys her life in Central Asia. "My happiness and attitude about being here make a big difference in how healthy my kids are."

8 Misadventures in Language Learning

"My husband comes by languages easily," explains Kathleen,[*] a mother of teenagers, just finishing her first year in Central Asia.

On the family's month-long visit to the field to check things out before they moved overseas, he was the one who picked up the most language. So before they left home, they told their friends how to pray: Peter would probably be able to function in the local language at the end of a year, but Kathleen might really struggle. "Pray for Kathleen!" they said. It turned out to be harder than they expected—for both of them.

Why have things been so hard? "Partly it's probably just an attempt by the enemy to derail us," Kathleen explains. "Partly it's that local teaching styles are not the best for our learning."

Like most church-planting teams in the region, Peter and Kathleen's team tries to limit newcomers' work and ministry investments for the first year so they can enjoy the local culture and get a good start on learning to speak the language. But because of some unexpected changes on their church-planting team, both Kathleen and Peter began work at their development agency's office long before the time designated for full-time language learning was over. "Then," pipes up ten-year-old daughter Cassie, "Dad became team leader and office director!"

Did Peter learn the language faster than Kathleen, as they expected? It happens often. Even if they have equal abilities, most wives tend to fall behind their husbands in learning the language. Often they are caring for small children or homeschooling and have less time for lessons, study, and practice. But for Peter and

---

[*] For more about Kathleen, see chapter 45. In This as a Family.

Kathleen, it turned out to be exactly the opposite. "Not what we expected at all," says Kathleen. "It's been easier for me because I'm a 'plodder.' I'm not moving fast, but I am moving and see steps of improvement."

Peter, who was sucked into work and had trouble keeping good language tutors, had the greater challenges. "Peter also learns in short bursts and needs higher accountability with language than I do. His struggle has been a real source of discouragement. This was such a surprise!"

Finding Language Teachers

In many frontier mission situations, formal language schools, classes, and printed materials in the local heart language are not available. Peter and Kathleen's team, like many others, responded to this reality by recommending language immersion on the field with one-on-one language tutoring.

Before Peter and Kathleen arrived in Central Asia, their team arranged for them to study with a local married couple who were experienced language teachers. When a major illness forced the couple to back out before lessons even began, Peter and Kathleen had to find something else. They didn't know how to find language teachers, or even where to look. When hopes of a language-immersion living situation did not pan out, the two felt the need for good language helpers even more strongly.

Kathleen's first language teacher, who knew some English, was also a new believer. "It wasn't just a teacher-student relationship. It was hard to know, 'Am I her student, or her friend? Am I supposed to be helping her grow?'" The girl was also under pressure from a controlling sister-in-law who did not want her to teach, so she was not always available for lessons.

Kathleen's second teacher was a girl from their aid-organization's office who spoke excellent English. "But that was a trap; we were always getting into these deep conversations in English!" Because of the tutor's circumstances, she wasn't able to help for long.

"The third, the one I have now, speaks no English, which can be hard. But she is an excellent teacher and also teaches at the local teacher's institute. She won't let me use 'borrowed' words (from the trade language), but really teaches me the local language." A young married woman who spends a lot of her time at home doing housework, Kathleen's teacher has an additional motivation: she enjoys the lessons as an opportunity to use her mind.

While others write their own lesson plans, Kathleen is glad to have a teacher who directs the learning. "It's been a real treat to work with her. She is gifted and has an unusual understanding of how people learn. We do grammar and vocabulary, and I always have homework and write stories using what I've been studying."

It has been much more difficult to find good language help for Peter. "Peter has had more language teachers than any foreigner we know! At first, he thought it would be better not to have a female teacher, which made things more difficult. He has been through the whole male staff of the English department at the institute. One guy would give him hard passages to read out loud. Peter would painfully work his way through it, and then the guy would call in his eight-year-old son and have him read it 'the right way.' That was so demoralizing!" With another teacher, Peter had to ask, "Would you please stop speaking English?" forty-five times in one lesson.

Now Peter has finally found a language tutor he can keep, someone who has time and interest in teaching. But will it last? Many of Peter's teachers have faced frequent or serious health problems that have disrupted language lessons, and this one is no exception. Earlier in the year she suffered through a bout of breast cancer. With the demands and ambiguity of life, it's hard to know from one day to the next whether a planned lesson will actually occur.

Practice and Progress

Peter and Kathleen have tried other ways to learn the language besides lessons. "We tried to use the LAMP method of language acquisition, but, like others in this setting, have not found it very successful." Kathleen adds, "My best language learning has come through house help. I have everyday contact and practice talking, and being corrected. That's part of the reason why I've been more successful than Peter; I have daily practice."

Kathleen can still write the local language far better than she can speak it. "I have lots of words in my head, but I can't get them out my lips! With time I can come up with what I need to say, but natural conversation is tough. I just need to keep working at it."

Looking back on their language struggles and other adjustments, Kathleen says, "Honestly, it's been a very tough first year. There were a lot of unplanned (and unprepared for) things that happened. It was a difficult year for our whole team, and for us. It's been one big learning curve. We are hoping that things will slowly keep getting better, especially leading up to our first furlough next year.

In the midst of her unexpected struggles, Kathleen has become somewhat philosophical. "The message God is creating in my heart is that he has called us to be faithful, not necessarily successful," she explains. "That's the hope that kept me going over this last year. That's what I cling to. If I can leave here having been faithful to what God had called me to, it doesn't matter how much I fail."

The same is true in her ministry efforts. "If all we can be right now is a family living in this neighborhood loving God, a light in the darkness, maybe that's all right. In some places you can raise up a whole new church plant in six months. You can't do that here.

"We are here for the long haul."

9 Ten Survival Tips for New Workers

Maryanne, a South African, served for several years in the Middle East as a single woman, and then she married a man who was part of a church-planting team in Central Asia. After several years of fruitful ministry there, she and her husband felt led to start a team of their own. They now have two small children as well. Because of her experience on the field, Maryanne often has the opportunity to minister to new workers. When she does, she always shares the survival tips she first discovered in Myron Loss's book *Culture Shock: Dealing with Stress in Cross-Cultural Living.** Maryanne's own examples bring it all to life.

1. Set reasonable goals. "Marrying onto a church-planting team that was already up and running, and marrying an extrovert, I suddenly had all of his relationships with no chance to build up to things. Just keeping up with people took up all my time. Some people set goals for six months. Me, I usually set goals only one week at a time! I sit down with my husband, and we figure out what our schedules will be and when we will try to have guests. Then I can have a reasonable idea of what else I can get done."

2. Don't take yourself too seriously. "Learn to laugh at yourself. Sometimes this is a discipline! I try to block these embarrassing moment stories out of my mind . . . but here is one.

"Just a few days after we had arrived, I decided to make scones and give them to my new neighbors. My husband had bought us a new oven, and we did not know there was a crack in the glass door. As soon as it got hot, it exploded! At the same time a bee flew in through the open window and stung me—on the bottom! I managed to salvage a few of my scones and cook them

---

* This list is slightly adapted from the one found in Myron Loss' book.

as best as I could, but when I went to visit my neighbors—it was the strangest thing—not one of them was home!

"Then it was off to my language lesson. I had never been to the office, but my husband told me which bus to take and where to get off. The driver said something unintelligible, which turned out to be, 'Is anyone going [where I was going]? If not, I'm going to take a different route.' But I didn't understand. Finally when his route was done he had to take me, personally, back to the office.

"For all these things to happen on one day seemed like too much. But I decided it would be a good thing to laugh about. And rather than wait until I felt better about it, I'd laugh now. My neighbors laughed too!"

3. *Learn to extend grace to yourself.* "Focus on actually relaxing and enjoying the process, and not stressing because you aren't where you want to be yet. Just be happy about small steps. Remember that you are human.

"There's a new girl in the country who is praying to see ten people saved in her first year. I tell her we don't allow people to do spiritual work until they are happy in the culture. I gave her our cultural learning program and told her it may take her a year to get through it, but will be worth it. I think she'll still bang her head, but she needs to adjust and not be hard on herself."

4. *Don't be afraid of being different.* "In the beginning I tried to just live and die for the people here, but I burned out. I have all these great role models, but that doesn't mean I have to do everything the way they do it. Don't be afraid of being different. For example, we never seemed to have enough family time. So when we started our own team, we moved our worship gatherings to Friday night and gave ourselves all day Saturday to be together as a family. We found we needed that.

"Everyone has somewhat different needs; I need time alone and something creative to do. Someone else may really need a close local friend. We try to help our teammates figure out what they need and not assume we're all the same."

5. *Reduce your stress where possible.* "It wasn't so easy in the beginning, but with time I got a washing machine and someone to help me in the house. I decided to take one less language lesson

each week. I just looked at my life and tried to organize it rather than letting it run away with me. I've been so blessed by moving into a house with a yard, it's better for my kids than an apartment was. That's been a major stress reducer."

6. *Forgive yourself and forgive others.* "Forgiving is crucial for maintaining good emotional health. You will make mistakes. It's okay. And others are going to say and do things that make trouble for you too. Sometimes it will be your teammates or your husband, or your local friends and neighbors. They probably don't mean to hurt you!"

7. *Establish close relationships with people in the host culture.* "I found a local 'mother' the same age as my own, and she took me under her wing. She and her daughters were some of my closest friends. We just spent time together. And not just sitting drinking tea: I've found one of the best ways to build friendships with women is to cook together. You're doing something with your hands and you don't need to talk the whole time. When I first came I learned a new local dish every week!"

8. *Be thankful.* "Every day I try to think of things I've enjoyed or appreciated, and small areas of success, and give the credit where it is due, to God. My mentor back home told me that when she takes her bath each night she tries to think of three things she is thankful for. It seemed like a good idea—plus I love to take baths!—so I do the same thing now."

9. *Be an encourager.* "That may be one of the best things you can do. We all need encouragement so much. Our previous team did not do much informally, but had formal times of affirmation when they wrote letters to each other, and when we left they all wrote out their blessings to send with us. Encouraging is good, if for no other reason than to get your eyes off yourself!"

10. *Take courage—someone understands.* "Our experiences are not all the same, but someone else has been through what you have before you—and survived it! You are not alone. If nobody else seems to know what you are going through, though, turn to the Lord, who always understands and has mercy on you."

❀ Ten Survival Tips for New Workers

10   What Keeps Her Going

Linda,* a young woman whose husband leads a church-planting team, has lived in Central Asia for about three years. She and her husband, Aaron, came to the field with no children, and have been able to invest heavily in language and culture study and relationship building. "Coming to the field together as a couple without kids was easier than coming as a single or family," says Linda. "Because we had no kids, I was free to pour myself into things; and because I have Aaron, I wasn't lonely!"

When she and Aaron decided to marry, they were eager to come to Central Asia as soon as they could, but planning for a wedding and adjusting to marriage took time. Moreover, their agency requires newlyweds to take the time to adjust to married life off the field instead of letting them go overseas right away. "Marriage is such an adjustment itself," says Linda. "Why adjust to that at the same time as adjusting to the field?"

Linda is glad they took some time to make sure their marriage was strong before moving to Central Asia. "I have a wonderful husband. I love just being with him. I love going visiting together and watching him interact with people. I love how he can always steer the conversation to the gospel and come across with such compassion and genuine caring."

Aaron's tenderness toward her touches Linda, too. Getting through the winter without fruits and vegetables, as most people do when the prices start to skyrocket, has been hard on Linda. "Sometimes Aaron will bring me home just one tomato! He's so

---

* For more about Linda, see chapter 32. Evaluating Cultural Values.

     Adjustment and Perserverance

good to me!" Linda says with a laugh. "I don't think I'm the kind of person that could do well here without a husband."

In addition to relationships with her husband and teammates, Linda says her relationship with Laura, a woman her age who ministers in a nearby city, helps her persevere. Linda and Laura make no excuses for taking the time to visit each other once a month; Laura is Linda's closest Western friend in the country. In some ways it is better that they serve on different ministry teams and can speak more freely about questions and frustrations than they might otherwise, as well as give each other advice.

Visitors from Home

Many teams restrict the number of guests from home that team members receive during the early years on the field, but in their three years in Central Asia, Linda and Aaron have had a surprising number of visits from family and friends, which has been encouraging. Not every visit is positive, but most of them are. "When people from home come and see us, if they have the right attitude and are here to encourage, that can be wonderful. Most of the short-term teams that have come have been so good! It's also a compliment to us when our visitors engage in society, for example being willing to wear a scarf when we go to the village in order to identify with me, because that's what I do."

Visiting the field can open up a family member or supporter's eyes to what life is really like for someone like Linda. "When people write us letters, you can tell the difference between those who have come to visit and those who haven't," she says.

Linda's team was recently blessed by a visit from a supporting church in another country. Because their home country's economy is in bad shape, Linda's team was struggling to pay for the completion of an important building project. The supporting church provided several thousand dollars necessary to finish the project, and even sent a short-term team to help.

"They sent their top people to come and teach several seminars in our development center," says Linda. "Because the members of the group were older, the trip was a bit of a stretch for them physically, but they thought we were wonderful and really wanted to minister to us however they could. They understood our difficulties and became like grandparents to us!"

The encouraging words of her husband and Western friends and visitors, however, do not carry as much weight as positive feedback from local friends. In the local culture criticism, though often constructive, flows freely. So receiving a compliment on Linda's ability to speak the local language seems like gold. "Neither Aaron nor I were good in school, but we believe God will equip you for what you're going to do," she explains. "It's encouraging when someone recognizes how far I've come." When local friends and neighbors point out how "Central Asian" she has become or praise her to her husband, Linda feels encouraged.

Making Local Friends

Now expecting her first baby, Linda has been surrounded by a group of local women who consider themselves honorary grandmothers to her unborn child. One is the house helper, Rachel, whom Linda has hired to help her prepare for motherhood. Rachel is a new believer. She and Linda often spend as much time talking about personal and spiritual things as doing housework. Often they study the Word with one another. Linda learns as much in these times as Rachel does, and her hope of studying the Bible with more local women in the years to come motivates Linda to press on. "Making a difference in people's lives and seeing them thrive, that's what excites me and keeps me going!"

In addition to Rachel, Linda spends a lot of time with a woman named Martha. Martha, who lives next to the office where Linda and her husband work and keeps an eye on the building for them, has become Linda's local mother. She looks out for Linda and helps her. "One day a family we had lived with in another city showed up here unannounced. We had not seen them for two years! It was terrible timing, though: we were on our way out the door and had three birthday parties to attend. Anyway, they came to the office first, and instead of sending them to us, Martha greeted them and took charge. She phoned us to see what we wanted to do. Then she invited them into her guest room. When I showed up, she was entertaining my guests!"

Linda admits she and Martha do not always see eye to eye: "She has her superstitions and funny things she tells me to do, but we genuinely love each other. She would do anything for me. I would leave my baby with her overnight," Linda adds with a laugh, "and I would not say that about many people. They have their own ideas about what is best." Like many Western women, she is not sure what to make of local childrearing practices. "But I know Martha will do what I want her to do."

Relationships like the ones she has with Rachel and Martha really add to the quality of Linda's life and her motivation to stay and reach out to the women around her. "It's nice to have some friends I don't have to put on airs and graces for. I'd say I have six to ten friendships like that now. I don't want relationships with people who are going to frown on me all the time." When she does face rejection or judgment from others in the community, she says, "Having some good friends helps!

"I love it when Rachel or Martha calls me their daughter or tells someone else I'm their daughter or sister. Just the fact that you've become friends with someone cross-culturally to the point where they accept you is amazing to me!" says Linda. "For our first two years, we focused on adaptation to the language and the culture. To see the fruit of it, and know that these relationships are the reason we made the investment . . . it's wonderful; it pays off."

Hopes for the Future

Aaron and Linda and their team are not seeing a booming ministry, not yet. Linda has not seen anyone come to faith. That would be a rare thing in this setting, at least so far. But the hope of people in the community putting faith in Christ encourages Linda and Aaron to press on. Linda is currently discipling a group of local believing women. Recently the group had a meeting to which each of the believers invited a friend she had been praying for and witnessing to. Linda was so thrilled to see her disciples reaching out. Then, at the last minute, every one of the local women who had said they would come made an excuse to stay away. "It was the most discouraging thing!" says Linda. Like many others ministering in the Muslim world, she finds her work is three steps forward, two steps back.

After three years on the field, however, she recognizes that true fruit is building relationships. Some of those relationships strengthen and encourage her and give her hope of what is to come. With that encouragement, she can keep reaching out to those around her. When things are hard, a good friend makes all the difference in the world.

"None of the physical things about living here really set me back or forward," says Linda. "It's relationships. That and the dream of a stable local church, that's what keeps us going."

11 Looking Forward to Going Back

Isabelle* has been part of a church-planting team in Central Asia for four years and is now enjoying her second furlough back in America, her home country. Her experience, like that of most others, is that furlough is both refreshing and draining. One aspect that has been both is reconnecting with family members. Isabelle's parents have divorced since she moved overseas, and her mother has remarried. What it means to come *home* to her family continues to evolve; and that can be disappointing and draining. Some things about the furlough are simpler for Isabelle than most missionaries because she is single. But she's also been spending time with a special new man in her life with whom she might have a long-term relationship; and that brings challenges of its own.

Many things have been great about this furlough, says Isabelle. "Just having good times with single girlfriends and laughing about stuff has been great. Just to hang out with friends and talk about things. There are no other single girls on our team."

The protected private time has been another nice thing about her furlough. "Here I can take a whole day just to relax much easier than I can there. I know people aren't going to be knocking on my door any minute. Even when they're not at my door, it's hard to relax entirely knowing there are Central Asians out there I could be talking to." She has also appreciated not being so closely watched and having to agonize over every decision and every purchase. In Central Asia her life is very public. Anything she owns is something people might ask to borrow, and they will

---

* For more about Isabelle, see chapter 2. Cultural Immersion, 41. Who Will Listen to a Single Woman? and 53. One-Room Schoolhouse.

certainly ask how much she spent. These things require careful thought and may drain Isabelle's energy—energy she can direct to other things while she's in America.

Missing Central Asian Ways

On the other hand, says Isabelle, she's learned to see many ways in which the Central Asian approach to life is better. "I'm learning to be relational and community-minded. The borrowing and lending thing really helps you let go of your possessions! And Central Asians just think differently. My tendency, when I need something, is to think, 'How I can take care of it myself?' Central Asians would say, 'How can I include other people?' I want to think that way more and not see people as interruptions. In Central Asia the thinking is, 'Of course, you are a person! Why wouldn't we want you here?'"

Some of the things Isabelle misses about Central Asia are simple and concrete. "I'm looking forward to wearing my Central Asian clothes: more dresses and all the exotic fabrics and glittery colors. I miss the food; I hope they make me my favorite dishes when I get back!" says Isabelle, licking her lips. "Melons will be in season; I'm looking forward to that. And I have a new eggplant salad I want to make!"

"And, yes, I miss Nescafé!" says Isabelle, smiling. The instant coffee brand popular in her region seems even more special because of the scarcity of other indulgences. "It's no fun to go shopping in Central Asia, not at the bazaar, and we have no Starbucks! If I'm having a bad day, the best thing I can do is come home and have Nescafé." Isabelle looks forward to a life with simpler pleasures.

Missing Her Team

Many of the things she misses go deeper. "I'm also looking forward to returning to community with the team. In the States if you are struggling, sometimes the tendency is toward being independent. You think it's wrong to burden others with your problems. You may tell them once or twice about something, but you don't want to bring it up on a continual basis. You think,

'I need to take care of myself; people have their own lives, so I shouldn't make them carry me and my problems.'"

In what has been a hard term for Isabelle, she has found true community with her team. She has been struggling, emotionally and spiritually. Some of it has had to do with her feelings about being single, and she's been trying to sort it out in her heart. "I have felt very weak, like I didn't have much to give the team. It was such a blessing to see these super people like Trent and Vivian say, 'Look, if it takes you two months, or six months, it doesn't matter; we want to work through this with you.' At one point there was something going on, a problem, and after the second or third time it happened I did not bring it up with them. I waited until it was over and I could say, 'This came up again, and here's how I dealt with it this time.' Vivian said, 'You should have let the team know! Whether it's the first time or the fifth time, we are here to bear each other's burdens.'"

Isabelle really appreciates her team's concern and willingness to walk with her through the hard times. "It was a new way of feeling loved and validated for me. I think I grew up thinking that it's wrong to feel bad. To see that feeling bad is okay gave me such a sense of security and value."

Dying to Self

Isabelle is also looking forward to going back to a way of life that forces her to die to herself, trust God, and live for others. This is something she could do without living overseas, but she would definitely have to swim upstream. As a missionary she has accountability and support for living a more sacrificial life. "I'm looking forward to things being a little harder," she explains.

"Even though we preach in our Western churches that you are not the center of the world, so much in our society is catered to 'having it your way.' Over there you get so used to inconvenience; you see that God is more interested in how you respond than in having things go your way. I really see the value of suffering now. I've seen through experience that when you die to yourself, what happens may bring you a lot of joy. I did not take too many opportunities for that when I lived in the States, but in Central Asia it's forced on you!"

God has used the hardships in Isabelle's life to help her learn to die to herself; as a result, she can't regret the life she has chosen or run from the trials she faces. She was thinking about this one day during her furlough when she went river rafting with some friends. "The water was quite low, but we had a guide who was really confident in his abilities. He rarely gets 'swimmers,' people falling out of the boat. He told us that when going through the rapids, most people avoid the rocks, but the best way to do it is to head right for the rocks—some of them, anyway. They would slow us down and help us get to the next place we need to go.

"I feel like God works that way. He's the experienced guide; he knows which rocks will destroy us and which ones won't. We have to trust him to use those rocks, and that they are what we need to get to the next place." For example, says Isabelle, "Being single can be seen as a rock, or as an opportunity." Talking about her life, even the hard parts, can help her build relationships with those around her. Admitting that as a single woman she gets lonely helps others reach out to her. If she shares her pain with someone else, she may not be giving them a burden, but a gift.

It may break Isabelle's pride when Central Asians see that she doesn't have it all together and they have to help her out. Sometimes they lecture her about the things she is doing wrong. They may nag her about not doing her share to keep the hallway of the apartment building swept and clean, or tease her over language and culture mistakes. Those may be "rocks" she'd like to avoid. But, as she explains, cultural knowledge is the one thing her Central Asian friends know they have that she does not. From their perspective she seems to have everything else: wealth, freedom, and opportunities. But there is one way in which they have the upper hand. "They are fluent in the culture, and I am not, and I shouldn't take it away from them. It's good that I should be the one who has something to receive." Exposing herself to the correction of others may be just the thing to help her win love and respect and come to better understand the people she is serving. It is all part of "dying to self."

Hopes for Upcoming Ministry

As she returns to Central Asia, Isabelle hopes to continue growing in her personal maturity and ability to minister wisely. "I've struggled with saying yes too often, or not knowing which opportunity to take. In his book *Ordering Your Private World,* Gordon MacDonald talks about living as a *called* person, and not a *driven* person. You can be driven by others or your expectations of yourself, maybe because you take pride or have your identity in the things you do. The book is about how not to be driven by those things, but by the glory of God."

However, after becoming fairly well adjusted to her team, host culture, and ministry, Isabelle is ready to make a few more small, strategic investments. "I see into people pretty easily and am interested in how their hearts are doing. So I want to take more roles at that level, for our team: really checking how people are doing and encouraging personal development. I want to make sure that even within the church-planting context, which is very focused on task, our hearts are alive and okay."

She also wants to look for new ways to minister to children, including the kids of her teammates and those of local believers. "I relate to kids in any culture, and they connect with me. These kids are a generation away from being the next church leaders! What can we be doing to prepare them? Even with the unbelieving kids, they are a generation away from being the next leaders of the country."

Returning from this furlough Isabelle will face some new challenges. For example, she has always faced questions about being single and when she is going to get married and to whom. How will her Central Asian friends respond now that she has a boyfriend in America? What does it mean to talk about this with close Muslim friends in a way that is honest and appropriate? "I'm probably going to have to deal with what people say about my boyfriend; my Central Asian family knows about him. I told them about the relationship to keep them from bringing other boys to me! I'm not too concerned about what they will say, but we'll see.

There are things to think about." Meanwhile, she's eager to get back to Central Asia.

Discussion Questions for Part 1

Chapter 1: Pajamas in Perspective

1. As you reach out to people in your host culture, what are some of the groups you could potentially identify with?

2. What are the different paths chosen by other missionaries in your host culture?

3. How do these choices seem to have affected the fruit of their ministry?

4. What are some of the challenging or satisfying things about laying down your identity for a new one?

Chapter 2: Cultural Immersion

1. What do you see as advantages and disadvantages of living with a local family?

2. Is this something you would consider for yourself? Why or why not?

3. If you are on the field, what are some things you have learned to appreciate about your host culture?

4. How has living cross-culturally changed the way you see yourself?

Chapter 3: Loneliness and Adjustment

1. If you are on your way to the field, what are some of your fears? If you are already on the field, do you remember some of the things you were afraid of when you first came?

2. Who can or did you ask to pray about these things?

3. How is God meeting you in these areas?

Chapter 4: Are We Staying or Going?

1. What was your path to the field?

2. What has helped you to accept your calling when things were tough?

3. What do you think are your needs for "down time"?

4. Do you feel like you are still in survival mode, or do you have a vision for what is to come? If so, what was the turning point?

Chapter 5: Those Who Persevere

1. If you are not yet on the field, what is your picture of what it will be like? If you are already there, what did you picture before you came, and how realistic was this?

2. How do you tend to view the Western church and its commitment to missions? What has shaped this view?

3. Have your timelines for language learning, ministry effectiveness, and even being able to stay on the field been interrupted? How have you responded to setbacks and changes? What has helped you?

Chapter 6: Marrying In

1. If you are married, do you and your husband have different amounts or types of cross-cultural experience? How do you respond to that?

2. When have you felt behind or divided from your husband's ministry? Do you have other friends who have faced or are facing similar challenges?

3. Do you know anyone in Daniel's position, who began his ministry before his marriage? What can you do to help the single missionaries you know or who serve on your team when they begin married life?

Chapter 7: Why Moms Should Learn the Language

1. How might—or did—your husband facilitate your learning of the local language? Do you think the approach Trent and Vivian took would work in your situation? Why or why not?

2. What do you think of Vivian's thoughts about the effect of a mother's language acquisition on her children? Have you seen families leave the field because of these issues?

Chapter 8: Misadventures in Language Learning

1. What has your past experience been with language learning? How well do you know what works for you?

2. To what extent have you been able to find the kind of language help you need?

3. What has God taught you through the discipline and sometimes discouragement of learning a new language?

Chapter 9: Ten Survival Tips for New Workers

1. Which one of these survival tips has been most important for you?

2. Are there any you disagree with or would consider lower priority?

3. Which one of these affects your area of greatest weakness or vulnerability?

4. What tips or examples would you add if you were giving advice to new workers?

Chapter 10: What Keeps Her Going

1. What four or five things keep you going?

2. How has God met your needs in surprising ways?

3. What can you do to seek out the things that will help you feel fruitful and content?

Chapter 11: Looking Forward to Going Back

1. What are things you like best about furlough times?

2. What challenges have you faced through furloughs?

3. What do you think it should look like for teammates to provide support and community for each other?

4. How have you seen God use trials you'd rather avoid to get you to a place where he can use you?

Part 2:
Relationships

How God Is Using Women to Touch
People around Them

12

God Gives Us Influence

As a single woman, Grace ministered to tribal communities in Southeast Asia for more than a decade before she married James and began working with Muslims. The Lord used her to help lead two villages to Christ during the years she was single. "I was very fulfilled and never thought about marriage," confesses Grace, whose parents had a difficult relationship. She did struggle with loneliness, and then stress, carrying the burden of ministry alone. "The lives of all these people I was working with seemed to be in my hands. I wondered if God should have brought a man to this work instead of me!" she says. "Though I didn't really want to give up my ministry and leave these people I loved. Then James came along. I thought maybe he could come help," she admits, "but I didn't see him as a husband!"

Getting married was not the last surprise she faced, of course. "I never thought I'd want to be a mom, either," says Grace, now the mother of three. "After we were married, James and I traveled too much to have a family right away. Even when we started having kids, I thought maybe we could split ministry and family fifty-fifty. But that's not the way the Lord would have it. I struggled about giving up an active ministry role, but in the end I laid it down. It's the Lord who resurrected it. James travels a lot, and I can't do that, but I can do other things." What does ministry look like for a woman who doesn't have an "active ministry role"?

God Brings People

With her life restricted by the needs of her kids, Grace finds it hard to reach out to others, but the Lord seems to bring people to her. Often times he uses her kids and their relationships to bring people into her life. When the mother of one of her son's kindergarten classmates asked for a Bible, Grace said, "'Come for lunch at my house so I can share with you. It will come more alive that way.' I shared the gospel with her, and she accepted Jesus! That gave me a lot of encouragement. As a single person, I could go where people were, and make things happen. I have only seen ten people saved since I was married, but my ministry didn't stop. God just brings you people, all the more when you can't get out as much. I can't think it's my doing; I see how God is doing do it."

Sometimes the Lord brings Grace ministry opportunities even when she resists them. A fellow believer tried to get her to spend time with a local friend, Sarah. "'Sarah really likes you. She loves to talk to you, and she's just become a Christian!' this sister said. Sarah was a new Christian, and I wasn't even interested, because I thought she was Chinese and my heart was for the Muslims," says Grace with a laugh. In a place like Southeast Asia, building networks of friendships among Muslims takes focus and a willingness to say no to other things. Sometimes that means saying no to spending time with non-Muslims.

Finally, Grace agreed to spend some time with Sarah. "'I want to ask you about tithing,' said Sarah. 'You know that I am a Muslim convert . . .' I was so surprised! Her father was a Muslim, and her mom Chinese. So she *is* a Muslim! We went out for coffee, and discipleship began." Grace was only one of the believers God used in Sarah's life. She had come to Christ in her home country in another part of Southeast Asia through some believers there. Then, her parents sent her away for school, hoping she would be under less Christian influence. But they chose to send her to America, where she met more Christians. Now, she lives in the same city as Grace. Experiences like this teach Grace what it really means that one person plants the seed, another waters it, but God is the one who makes things grow. Even as a busy mother, Grace can be part of the process.

Raising Kids among Muslims

For a while Grace's family lived in a Christian community where she enjoyed ministering to believers, but something in her was restless. "I wanted to be part of a non-Christian community. I wanted to raise my kids and teach them values amid non-Christians," she explains. Some of Grace's friends had a hard time understanding why she would want to leave the Christian community, "But it was the desire of my heart," she says simply.

Now they live in a community with a significant Muslim population, and Grace's three children attend a local school where many of the students and teachers are Muslim. At first many of her Christian friends were against this change. They didn't think Grace's children would get the best education in such an environment. It seems to be working out well, however, and Grace has enjoyed making friends with the Muslim moms whose children are her kids' classmates. This does not mean there are not tensions. Heidi, Grace's eleven-year-old daughter, is very popular with her Muslim friends and spends much time listening to music with them—music Grace is not so sure she approves of. She is a little worried that Heidi will be pulled away. And, because she studies all the time, Heidi has little time for Christian friends. "Heidi is the kind of person who goes deep in friendship. She will only have two or three friends, and is so busy with the girls at school."

Making Local Friendships

Many Muslims in Southeast Asia consider Christian households "unclean" and are reluctant to allow non-Muslims to visit in their homes, so Grace feels blessed that the friendships and influence God has given her have brought her invitations to homes as well as meetings, social events, and parties with influential Muslims in the community. Although the walls between them are coming down, Grace knows her life is still different from their lives. Last year she took a trip to the beach with a dozen Muslim women who had become friends of hers. As they began to talk about their marriages, Grace fell silent. She does not have the same problems they do. To say too much might emphasize the differences. "I said nothing, but just being there was good. This year when they started talking about another day at the beach, they said, 'We want to make sure we do it when you are here, Grace!'"

Another Muslim woman, Zelda, is the mother of one of her son's classmates. Her seven-year-old son suffers from leukemia, and Zelda has been saying prayers, seeing doctors, and doing whatever she can to help her son get better. Now the boy is beginning to open up and become more social, and his doctor asked what was making the difference. Zelda credited changes Grace has helped make at the school their boys attend. It is gratifying that someone notices. "The doctor says he wants to come visit and see what's making the difference!" Grace says.

Before Grace left the country on a furlough, she attended a birthday party for Zelda and was the only non-Muslim there. "'I'll miss you. You are one of my best friends,' Zelda told me," exclaims Grace in wonder. "I haven't actually spent that much time with this woman! It's in the spiritual realm these things happened." God seems to grant her favor and use her even when her time and energy seems so limited.

Another friend called Grace the night before she left on that furlough to report on an aging relative for whom Grace had been praying. "Grace, my uncle passed away last night," she said. "Then quickly she added, 'I love you, Grace!' and hung up the phone.

"I'm quite busy. That's my struggle. I don't have time for myself. I have to get up at six to get kids off to school, and I have all these meetings, and then they come home from school. After getting the kids to bed, I'm on the phone. Between kids and ministry, I don't have time. But God keeps opening the doors. When people see God's anointing on us, they won't let go of us!" Grace does seem to have much more influence in the lives of her friends than anyone would expect, but when asked about it she simply explains it is the power that comes from walking with God.

13 Loving Muslims in Her Own Country

Having grown up in a mono-cultural area of England and being happy in her career as a nurse, Joyce had no intention of becoming a missionary. She thought missionaries were people who went overseas, not people like her. She even made a deal with God: she would go to Bible college and give the Lord two years of ministry if she could go right back to her career when she was done. But that was before God opened her eyes to the opportunities to minister to Muslims right in England. Joyce, who is single, made a two-year commitment to a mission agency working in one of the most Muslim areas of the country. More than a dozen years have passed, and Joyce hasn't left yet.

Like many Muslim immigrant communities, those Joyce works with appear to be very closed and insular. They guard their cultural and religious identity in England more strongly than they might in their home countries. However, an insider's view is different. They are also a tremendously warm and hospitable people who have made Joyce a part of their families. "Now I have more than 100 women in my network: my students, their friends, and their kids," says Joyce. "It's like family." They invite her to special events, seek her advice, and tell her the kinds of secrets she can't imagine telling anyone.

Behind the Veil

One of the ways Joyce serves the immigrant community is to teach English to women in their homes. As word spreads about this ministry, she has had many requests for help. One came from a woman who lives above a small, storefront mosque nearby. Joyce walks past it every day on her way to the church where she works. "Kids would go there to read the Qur'an and learn Urdu, and women would go to learn Arabic. I knew some of the kids but not the adults. Then one of my students said, 'The woman who lives there would like you to come teach her English.'"

Joyce had never seen this woman, who lives in purdah (literally, "veiled" or in seclusion). This means she seldom leaves her home and then only with her face and body completely covered except for her eyes. "It was a wonderful opportunity for me to meet Karima. She is tremendously warm and open, and her husband, the imam [a Muslim priest], is too. At Easter he asked me, 'I'm sure Easter is not about chocolate; what's the real meaning?' and we were able to talk about it."

Joyce soon learned that the greatest tragedy in Karima's life is that she has not been able to have children. "She realizes I have my own pain and can identify with that," explains Joyce. Perhaps it is because Joyce is single and lives away from her parents that Karima knew Joyce understood suffering.

"Four or five years ago she felt that the shame of not having kids was not something her husband should have to face. So, with enormous generosity of spirit, Karima arranged another marriage for her husband. She found the woman herself. Her husband did not want it and cried at the wedding, he loved Karima so much. But the second wife came to live with them; they are all together, and now the husband and second wife have two children."

It may seem strange that polygamy occurs in modern Britain. Imagine what it would be like to share a small flat with your husband's other wife. Yet Joyce is impressed with the family's devotion, integrity, and commitment to one another and would love to see them come to know the Lord. "They are an amazing family. I've always felt that God has his hand on them. Can you imagine what the ripple effect will be like on the community if God changed their hearts? Absolutely everyone knows them, and there would be a tremendous cost for them to follow Christ; everyone would know about it."

Blessing and Cursing

Another aspect of ministry to which many British Christians are unaccustomed is the role of the spirit world. Many women Joyce knows live in the world of magic, spells, and curses that characterizes their culture in South Asia. "You don't want to be afraid of it, but you need to be aware. When someone is jealous of something—a child, car, or possession—cursing is a common problem. There are charms, black necklaces with little leather boxes and Qu'ranic words inside, to protect you against the evil eye," she says. "It's a real force to reckon with. People are jealous of what you have and what you are. People take the spirit world very seriously in this context."

Consider the experience of her long-time friend, Sharra. "She is one of my best friends anywhere, not just among Muslims," says Joyce. "Six years ago Sharra started having real struggles in her life. Things were flying around her house at night, a child's toy phone started talking, and her house filled with smoke when there was no fire. Her son was affected too: he was taking his clothes off and rolling around and talking in strange voices. Sharra, too; she would go into a trance-like state, groan, make terrible noises."

The probable source of Sharra's problems? A curse from her mother-in-law, who resents the younger woman. Joyce responds by bringing the presence of Jesus into the home. "I pray and go visit her and wait. I pray all the time before I go visit her, have people pray while I'm there, and when I leave I ask the Lord to cleanse me. I open the Scriptures daily and put on the armor! My feeling is that I cannot deliver her alone; I need to bring others, when she's ready for that." At one point, Joyce even brought people from the church to pray for her. Afterwards Sharra said she felt terrible. "'It's because Satan doesn't want to let go,' I told her, but she was terrified. She became agitated when I tried to talk about Jesus with her. But she has spent thousands of pounds on Muslim healers and holy water."

After seeing Sharra suffering so much and drawing back from the things of God, Joyce wept and began to despair. The problems in her friend's life seemed so devastating. Then God gave Joyce the picture of the prodigal son. In some ways Sharra has chosen the situation she is in. "'It's her decision, but she's in my hands,' says the Lord," explains Joyce.

A breakthrough both in Sharra's life and the immigrant ministry in general may be slow in coming. There are various stages of sowing seeds, clearing rocks, and preparing land. As a fellow missionary says of her, "Joyce is watering and softening the ground with her tears."

Relationships That Go Deeper

Karima and Sharra's problems are not uncommon, says Joyce. "Lots of women struggle with marital problems; there are a lot of drug issues here, and demonic problems that come from folk Islam. This all makes it very easy to get close to people and share with them on a heart level."

Although Sharra resists being prayed for, few other women do. "When they want me to pray for them, they don't mean, 'Pray for me when you go home or at church,' they mean 'Now, in Jesus' name, can we pray?' I don't know how it is in other places, but that kind of thing would not usually happen with the English! With these people, though, relationships go deep, and continue to deepen over the years."

By building relationships with women, letting them see how she really lives and the struggles she has, and praying and crying together, Joyce has not only expressed love to immigrant Muslim women, she has also found a family for herself.

Living a Holy Life

The Muslims Joyce works with are more direct in their questions of her than her own people, the English, would ever be, and that's taken some adjustment. Joyce is, of course, asked why she is not married. She tries to answer with honesty and grace. She also makes choices in her life to demonstrate that although she is single at an age when her Muslim friends would be well into marriage, she lives a life of holiness. She knows people are watching.

"I had a man in one of the shops I go to say, 'Can I ask you a question? Why is it that you never have dirty men in your house?' There are lots of prostitutes in the area and maybe people think they are Christians. I was really glad I have had a rule never to allow men alone with me in the house." She admits it can be inconvenient. Nice Christian men do not understand, sometimes.

Joyce recognizes that even if her singleness seems a disadvantage, it does not hold her back in a European context as much as it might elsewhere. "It would be very difficult for me as a single woman to go live in Kashmir, but God in his mercy brought them here. I believe they will be bearers of light to their own people."

Many believers who live in areas like Joyce's city that have large immigrant populations are afraid of making cultural mistakes, and offending or angering their Muslim neighbors. Others are simply afraid to talk to people who are different from them. But as Joyce says, "Love covers a load of sins and mistakes. People pick up that you really want to know them. I've never had a friendship break up over a mistake. People in the churches have the impression that Muslims are easily offended, but it's not really like that."

She has learned a few rules about proper behavior from her Muslim friends. "Take your cues from them," she says. "Don't stretch out your hand to shake hands with a man or make eye contact with men. Instead, slightly avert your gaze and be reserved. Be friendly, say hello, and smile, but only with other women."

Like many other missionaries, Joyce has reached the stage where the ministry opportunities open to her exceed her capacity. Women beg her to come into their homes, to be their friend, and to help them with English. But Joyce has too much on her plate. "I have to say no the majority of the time. I cannot give my heart to any more than I already have, not at the level they want. Pray and ask God to raise up more workers."

14 A Place for Broken People

Joan and her husband Matt have been living and serving in Central Asia for almost ten years—years full of incredible highs and lows. "But how could I want anything else out of life?" Joan feels that the breaking and healing process she went through in her early years on the field were the best preparation she could have had. They taught her lessons she did not know she needed to learn.

"Before I went to the field, I thought I was relatively healthy," Joan says wryly. "We were youth pastors and got all kinds of affirmation from the church and from the parents." She thought she was great and was ready to put her ministry skills to work in a new place. "Then we went to the field and had almost no affirmation for two years." That kind of experience can be quite humbling. Team conflicts left further wounds. God used those to bring Joan's problems and insecurities to the surface.

"I knew the Lord was doing something, so I put myself into every situation I could find where I could get healing from God. I found myself at prayer meetings and conferences screaming, shaking, and crying. It was a five-year process, and it was hard. Now I know the reason. God was doing what he wanted in me so I could be a healer of the nations. You wouldn't believe how many hurting people are out there!"

Joan is amazed by the pain she sees in the lives of the believers she works with in her city's fledgling church. Many have come through all kinds of abuse and rejection, problems that do not simply go away when they come to Christ. "People will come to the cell group meetings barely crawling through the door. 'God, just get me through this week!' they are saying, and they get enough to get through that week. When you bring people like that to Jesus, it's what they live for."

Relationships

Valerie

Valerie is a friend of Joan's who also needed to experience healing. For generations, the women in Valerie's family have been hurt deeply. Her grandmother gave birth to twelve children, and eleven of them died. Valerie's mother, the twelfth, was a victim of the Central Asian "bride-stealing" practice in which young girls are kidnapped by young men, raped, and taken into the men's families. Valerie's mother was kidnapped while walking to school. Fear and loss at losing her last living child drove Valerie's grandmother to all kinds of witchcraft and occultism, and this became a regular part of the lives of Valerie's family.

When Valerie reached her late teens, families came around trying to arrange a marriage with her. One man's family was particularly insistent. "Please don't make me marry him!" Valerie pleaded. But the other family, also involved in the occult, put a spell on her. She was in a fog and didn't know what was going on—but she woke up married. "That kind of thing happens; they put curses on people to make them do what they want," explains Joan sadly.

Valerie's new husband turned out to be a raging alcoholic, and he beat her terribly. After several years, she began to sleep in the outhouse or wander the streets at night to get away from him. She wouldn't leave him, however, because she felt so much shame. Also, she was afraid he would kill her.

Valerie's mother, who had also suffered greatly in her marriage, told her, "The reason your husband is abusing you is because you are not a good enough Muslim." So Valerie began dressing even more religiously, saying more prayers, and doing everything a good Muslim is supposed to do. It did not seem to help. "She was working as a housekeeper for some Christian friends of mine," says Joan. "They wanted to minister to her, but she didn't want 'infidels' to pray for her. At one point her husband actually went to church and got a Bible. She tore it up and put a curse on him to keep him from reading.

"Whenever I saw her during this time," Joan adds, "Valerie says I told her, 'You are so beautiful! You are so precious to God.'

I don't remember ever saying that. I think the Lord knew what she needed, and that's what he allowed her to hear."

Joan often invited Valerie to visit a cell group, but she always said no. Finally, Valerie allowed Joan's friend to pray for her. Through that, God touched her and she began searching for him. Eventually she did visit a cell group. She said she saw Jesus on the faces of all the women there.

The Healed Become Healers

Just as the Lord had shown Joan his love and compassion, healed her, and enabled her to minister to Valerie, he healed Valerie to equip her to minister to others. Joan and Matt had begun a counseling ministry that helps their local friends recognize and come to terms with the wounds and deceptions that have shaped their lives. As Valerie was transformed, she went on to join Joan in this ministry.

"Valerie let God show her the lies she had believed and bring truth into her life. Now God is using this abused, downtrodden, oppressed housekeeper in his church! She is the most anointed counselor I've met! And do you know what she says to these women? She says, 'God loves you. You are so beautiful, and you are so precious to him!'"

When the country next door opened up, Valerie was one of the first to go in with the gospel. "Some of the other Christians were saying, 'You can't send local believers there; they will be murdered! But she is so passionate. She wanted to go. Valerie and I and another woman took a trip there, and it was one of the best times of my life! Valerie ministered to everybody, even the guards at the border. One of them had been in a war zone for seven years and must have spent an hour pouring out his heart to Valerie.

"We went to a remote village that never has contact with the outside world. Sixty percent of the people are opium addicted; they even give drugs to their babies. All the babies are so small and feeble, and the people don't understand why; nobody has ever told them. Valerie ministered to them and taught them how to take care of their families. She wants to see these women healed!

"I am so thankful I get to see God moving like that, and to

be a small part of it. God healed me so I can heal her and she can heal countless others. He blesses us in ways we never could have dreamed of!"

Meg

Meg, another local friend of Joan's, was stolen to be a bride at fifteen. From everyone else's perspective she disappeared from the face of the earth. Without a passport, she wasn't technically a citizen. Her husband turned out to be a drug addict and landed in prison. Meg had to feed her children, so she began to farm. When her husband got out of prison, he would steal her crops and sell them to get money for drugs. Believers prayed for this deeply wounded and discouraged woman. In fact, Joan's friend Valerie and her eight-year-old daughter were among those who would pray for and minister to Meg while she sobbed.

"Meg has been transformed into a beautiful flower; I don't know how else to describe it. When we left on furlough, she came to the goodbye party. She sang a beautiful song for each of the women, laying her hands on them and singing about what God had put inside each one of them. She's just a plain, simple woman. But her song—I didn't know that was inside of her!

"I love being part of this, seeing local friends draw out gifts in others, and in us! God is so good. If you let him take you where he wants to take you, there will be hard times, but he uses everything. Everything."

15 Bringing the Gospel of Peace

"The woman who lived across the street from us had married into a poor family with five sons," says Vivian.* "The mother-in-law made her life pretty difficult, so she'd come over and hang out at our place and have something to eat." As a result, Vivian built a relationship with her Central Asian neighbor, Bonnie, and Bonnie's husband, Josh.

"I felt so burdened by this family. They were not good Muslims, they were generally ungodly people, and they fought all the time. It was a very unhappy household. So I thought, why don't I just take Matthew 10:28–30 to them and offer them a new way? Jesus says, 'Come to me, all you who are weary and burdened, and I will give you rest.' So I went, bringing two copies of the gospel of Luke."

Two Responses

"First I went to the mother-in-law's room. After I shared the verses with her she said, 'You know the way to get to heaven? There's a bridge over a chasm, and if we say our prayers five times a day we can cross it. . . .' She just gave me the whole Muslim line. It seemed like a closed door. Later I saw cuttings of the gospel of Luke I had given her in the toilet paper trash and dropped in the street. That showed me how un-Muslim they were; good Muslims would never cut up a holy book!

"I left her room, went across the yard to Josh and Bonnie's room, and said the exact same things to Bonnie. But her response

* For more about Vivian, see chapter 1. Pajamas in Perspective, 7. Why Moms Should Learn the Language, 18. A Troubled Believer, 20. Jesus in the Hospital Ward, 23. Available in the Busiest Season, 42. Even a Healthy Marriage . . . , and 53. One-Room Schoolhouse.

was completely different. 'How do we come to Jesus?' was her question. 'Well, read his words here, and in doing that you are coming to him,' I told her. 'He'll lead you where to go next.' So she started to read the Scriptures. This was all in October or November."

Vivian and her family had made a tradition of using Christmas and Easter events to bless their Muslim friends, build relationship with them, and, to some degree, testify of their faith. As Christmas approached they decided to have a party. They had planned a little program and invited different people in the neighborhood to read parts of the Christmas story. One of those who came was Bonnie. A Central Asian believer from the capital city had come to the party and was preaching the gospel. As Bonnie listened, she was amazed. Listen to him talk! she thought. And he wasn't even a foreigner; in her eyes, he was "one of us."

Bonnie found Vivian at the party and asked, "What if I wanted to receive Christ? My husband and all of them would be against it. Would I have to tell them right away?" The believer from the capital city advised her to take three months to pray for them and grow in her own understanding. By that time she would know better what to tell them and could see if it was the right time. So she went home and, in her own room that night, received Christ.

Not telling the family seemed like a good plan, but it didn't work. As Vivian says, "She's such a talker, of course, that she couldn't 'not tell'! The family was pretty upset at us for a while. Someone told us later about a story on the radio about a local family whose daughter-in-law had been made into a Christian by foreigners, that it had caused division in the family and was a terrible thing. It could have been this family. I wondered if that was their view of what happened. Actually, the family was quite a mess long before, full of problems and divisions. Bonnie coming to Christ did more to help than hurt the family in that it gave her the encouragement to stick it out as a daughter-in-law."

As a believer, Bonnie now had the peace of Christ in her heart.

Finding Community

Both Bonnie and her husband had studied in the capital and preferred the regional language, Russian, over the local language. "We thought if they did come to Christ," Vivian says, "they'd respond better in a Russian church. My husband even gave them a Russian Bible, but we later found out they didn't touch it because it was a Russian thing!" Like many Central Asian Muslims, Bonnie and Josh held tightly to their ethnic identity—even though they were not comfortable with the language.

Trent and Vivian were skeptical about seeing Bonnie and Josh, who also came to Christ, join the emerging fellowship of Muslim-background believers. The young couple's more modern values and preference for the Russian language might clash with the culture of the emerging local church and cause confusion all around. But Josh and Bonnie knew that joining a Russian fellowship might keep the gospel from spreading within their family. "'Our family will never come to Christ,' they said. 'They won't realize it's for our people.'"

Years later, Josh and Bonnie are still walking with Christ and finding fellowship with local believers, both Russian and Central Asian. Since then, Josh and Bonnie have been able to get an apartment of their own, so they don't have to live with Josh's difficult mother, though they must still seek ways to show her respect. Bonnie's sister and mother, on the other hand, have both come to Christ.

16

An Abundance of Friendships

Seven years have passed since Jennifer* and her husband came to live in Central Asia where they are part of a church-planting team. Now they have two young children, a good team, and many local friends. In fact, by their second year, Jennifer had more relationships than she could deal with. Though that brought challenges of its own, it was the answer to Jennifer's fervent prayers.

When she left America, Jennifer left behind her best friend, Heather. She didn't know that her husband, Robert, was secretly praying for a local "Heather." When the first Central Asian woman they met proved to be a soul mate for Jennifer, they knew God had answered both their prayers. While their early teammates were kind and friendly, they were from a more reserved culture and couldn't meet Jennifer's needs for warmth and affection. Her new soul mate could. "Hannah would come and lay her head on my lap," says Jennifer. "She was really warm and loving."

College Girls

Looking around for other friends, for their first year on the field Jennifer and her family were happy to invite a couple of college-aged girls to move in. This was not an unusual situation in their host culture. Living with a family is safer and more pleasant than staying in a dormitory, so it's not unusual for village girls to live with a local family when they come to the city to study. Frequently Jennifer and the girls would stay up late talking into the night. What they were talking about Jennifer couldn't say, because she was just starting to learn the language, but it certainly

---

* For more about Jennifer, see chapter 22. The Cost of Compassion, 30. Suddenly Rich, and 50. The Perils of Parenting Preschoolers.

motivated her to keep studying! By the end of their year in the house, one of the two girls had received Christ.

Loneliness may be an inevitable aspect of adjusting to the field, but not all workers find themselves alone. During their first term Jennifer estimates they received more than forty guests a week. They still do a lot of entertaining, although they had to cut way back when Jennifer developed a chronic illness. Whereas initially they collected relationships almost randomly, now they focus on the people they want to really invest in.

The first pair of girls who lived with their family worked out so well that Robert and Jennifer were open to more. When ten young women showed up at their door hoping to be the ones, they chose two. This time, however, what started as company for Jennifer quickly turned into a busy ministry of discipleship. A natural evangelist, Jennifer had shared her testimony with them right away. The second day they were there, one of the girls got a bad headache. "I so wanted to pray for her!" says Jennifer. "I got my Bible and shared verses with her about Jesus healing people. Robert had just got home and he joined in. We prayed for her in Jesus' name. I'm not even sure if it was in English or in the local language. Her headache was healed.

"After we prayed she was just sitting there, stunned, still holding out her hands. The Lord had met her! She was just flooded with the Holy Spirit as we prayed. She had never felt that before. She ran into the other room where the other girl was cooking and told her what had happened, and she said, 'Pray for me too!'"

Jennifer and her husband shared the gospel with the girls using the New Testament, and the next day showed them the *Jesus* film. And so, after only three days in their home, both of the girls prayed with Jennifer and Robert to receive the Lord.

"We spent every evening doing discipleship. That's how our second year began!"

The Birth of a Ministry

"Ministry to the girls and their friends really took off, in spite of us. Or at least in spite of me," says Jennifer's husband, Robert. "I was thinking that having people live with us could get in the way of ministry. But God is so sovereign and wonderful, and so is my wife. Wonderful, I mean, not sovereign! One of those girls had great leadership gifts and potential. They shared the gospel with their friends, and people were coming to the Lord.

"In the beginning," Robert says, "we felt we should be reaching heads of households; what are girls? But early on God spoke to us that these girls would be doors to their families. So we began building relationships with their parents, which strengthened the girls' position and credibility as well. We would spend weekends with them in the village; we'd talk and pray and sing with them. So, by the time we'd been here two and a half years, there were twelve young women following the Lord."

"Ministering to them became our first priority. Stuff around the house just wasn't getting done," says Jennifer. "We'd have ten or twelve girls there for a Bible study in our house, and it would get to be 8:00. We'd all be starving, and no one would be making dinner. Meals here take at least an hour to prepare." Although Jennifer had done most of the cooking since her family came to the field, the girls who had lived with them the first year had pitched in quite a bit. The girls living with them the second year did not. One of them, the youngest in her family, was used to being taken care of and had a hard time seeing how to contribute.

Can You Have Too Many Relationships?

Eventually, Jennifer's family had to make a decision to hire a hard-working house helper and to limit hospitality. Because of her bubbly personality, compassion, and commitment to sowing broadly in friendship, this was difficult for Jennifer. "The reality is, you can say no. Our local friends don't have as many guests and demands as we do, and we've seen them say no, so we knew we could do it too.

"So now I handle invitations the same way others do. When they ask me to do something, I tell people, 'If I get permission, I'll come.' When I was sick Robert would not give me permission to do things, so it was his deal. I had wondered how to say no and be 'cultural,' and it worked. I was also convicted about the scriptural principle, 'Let your yes be yes and your no be no.' And in my heart I was often saying, 'No, no,' then at the door I'd say, 'Yes, come in.' I thought I was being 'cultural,' but it was a lie. I had to learn to be honest and let it show, instead of being a super missionary, bouncing around.

"It was a step of faith for me to put people into God's hands because I can't take care of them. We didn't have good relationships with many of the neighbors; they were using us and leeching from us. I had to seek the Lord about who to invest in: the Lord, my husband, the kids of course, and certain other people. We even had to put boundaries on the team as well, to tell them they needed to leave after team meetings instead of hanging out at our house."

While letting her husband be the "bad guy" and limiting her freedom keeps her from doing too much, Jennifer's house helper also protects her by answering the door and phone. "When I teach the kids, or meet with my prayer partner, or just need to spend time with the Lord or take a nap, she just takes care of things. She came to the Lord through one of the local believers. Someone else disciples her, not me."

Even as she is not able to build relationships with everyone, Jennifer is seeing her local friends believe in Christ and be equipped to minister to those she can't reach. "Robert and I decided we would stop whatever we were doing and pray for this one neighbor family every time we heard them having a fight. They fought all the time, so we were always praying! One day the wife heard me offer to pray for a neighbor's daughter, and she asked if she could bring her son over for me to pray for. I was amazed that the first time this woman came to my house was so I could pray! We asked the Holy Spirit to come on her. The next day she watched the *Jesus* film and received Christ.

"She is so on fire. We were surprised, but we shouldn't have been, considering we had been praying for her all the time! There are so many open women here, because they are so desperate. The other day I was sharing the gospel with another neighbor who said, 'Your words are so sweet. You should teach from house to house.' Well, it's this woman who should teach from house to house."

When they first came to the field, Jennifer and Robert and their team were constantly going out looking for contacts. But this is a different season. She still disciples leaders, shares the gospel, and prays with people, especially after her kids are in bed. But most of Jennifer's ministry happens in the house now. She doesn't get out as much. "Every now and then I need to grab a friend and get out. We'll go to a wedding just to dance!" she says, grinning. "It's a part of the culture I love."

17

Choosing Your Friendships

It's been seven years since Ann,* a single woman, first came to Southeast Asia as a church planter in a Muslim community. For her first five months, Ann lived in another part of the country with a family of Southeast Asian Christians. "It was very good for language and cultural awareness in a lot of ways, and it made my life a lot more focused. I spent the vast majority of time with Southeast Asians," she says. However, when the time came to an end, she was ready for the increased freedom and privacy that come from living alone or with other westerners: "Like being able to turn my computer on without it being a big deal," says Ann. "And to come and go whenever, not having to deal with coming home and finding fifteen people in the house for some reason or another."

When she moved into her host culture, God provided another living situation that also had its benefits. "For a period God gave me a delightful roommate from another mission agency. My personality is fairly serious, but Carla had a great sense of humor. It was a nice balance. And we worked well as a team. When you are dead tired and someone comes to the door, you can say, 'I'm going to my room and shutting the door; is that okay?' You can save each other on a lot of levels. We had different gifts too. Also, it made sense culturally. In Southeast Asia a single woman living alone just doesn't make sense. They can't figure it out. So for us to be together immediately relieves questions. The neighbors feel better. They don't have to worry about you. I liked it too. It can be quite lonely at night."

---

* For more about Ann, see chapter 29. Taking a Backseat to Local Believers and 40. Life and Leadership as a Single Woman.

Possessive Relationships

Ann, Carla, and their teammates began getting to know people in their new community. As they discovered, even in a culture of very friendly people it can be difficult to build or maintain the network of relationships necessary for an effective ministry. This may simply be because you are, in fact, behaving in a counter-cultural way. Most people in a traditional Muslim society are born into a large, dense network of relationships. In contrast, you are trying to build one. And you may not be following all the rules. Ann found that her local friends could not understand her relationship choices and the reasons behind them. They were jealous of the time she spent with others. Ann says it was like living in a fishbowl; she had no privacy. "Everyone could see how much time you were spending with different people."

After a while Ann and her teammates were able to pick up on why this might be. There was in fact a cultural value behind the attitude, and it wasn't just pettiness and selfishness. Ann explains: "We find it negative, in our culture, to have favorites; we build lots of relationships. But for them, favorites provide a real bond. So your friend doesn't understand what you are doing when you make other friends. She may think, 'If you are going to someone else, there's something in me that's not good enough.'"

Ann had to wrestle through a biblical response to this. In the end she concluded that she would not change her approach. "I'm here for something bigger than to just be your friend," she tried to tell her friends, gently. It doesn't always work. "You can explain, and they won't get it; they just have to accept it without understanding. The jealousy is there, and it's a negative thing. We don't want to single people out. So you keep telling them that you love them and that they mean a lot to you."

A Draining Friendship

One of the friendships in which Ann was deeply invested was her relationship with Lily. "I think Lily actually had some kind of illness like manic-depression. I have no idea for sure, but she was not healthy in relationships. Lily was demanding my presence and calling all the time." Sometimes Ann wanted to pull back, but she did not feel that she could. Lily seemed interested in the gospel. If Ann didn't give up on her, maybe Lily would become a believer. "Sometimes she was suicidal and said, 'If you don't come and see me these horrible things are going to happen.' I'd get this pit-in-my-stomach feeling around her. But I ended up feeling obligated to maintain the relationship because she was really seeking God.

"There were a couple of sources of release," says Ann. Ann wrote and asked friends and supporters to pray for her in this situation and received advice from several quarters. A friend who was a counselor told her it sounded like Lily might have borderline personality disorder. That was not something Ann could fix just by loving Lily. Reading *Boundaries* by Henry Cloud and John Townsend helped Ann see that it was okay for her to put some distance into the relationship. She gave herself permission to keep phone calls with Lily short, and only talked to her for an extended period once a week. She did not try to explain what she was doing to Lily, just trusted that God would supply the rest of what her friend needed in other ways.

The decision seems to have paid off. "God has met her. I've seen tremendous changes. I've been a constant in her life over time, and I've been able to give her intense time when I chose to, instead of all the time or when she chose. The relationship has been—well, I don't feel guilty anymore. She was depending too much on me. Someone with borderline personality, if that's what it is, gets their identity from other people. When I backed off, I was still there so she could not say I had abandoned her, but she found some help in God. She is still not a Christian, but she has fallen in love with 1 Corinthians 13. She memorizes these verses and holds them dear."

Finding Friends to Have Fun With

Her relationships with Lily and other challenging people took a toll on Ann. "If you don't like your relationships they get you into a burnout situation. Someone even said to me, 'Pick and choose the relationships you like!' It was not like me; I tend to have a plan and stick with it. I was trying to go see my neighbors

Relationships

every day, and that seemed strategic but was a lot less fulfilling. Then I saw that it was okay, for example, to go hang out with university girls and have fun." It was important, even for a serious person like Ann, to have someone to be silly with now and then.

Part of what helped release Ann from the standards she had set for herself was the example of her roommate Carla. "She had an approach that was different. 'I'm going to go do this instead because it's more fun!' she'd say. 'You can't do that, do something just because it's fun, can you?' I wondered. 'Why not?' she said. She had a blast with people. That helped me see I needed to rethink it. I was trying to do everything in this tight circle in the neighborhood, and she just went off with the people she clicked with. And the relationships went deeper!"

Ann still had some relationships with demanding women who tried to make her feel guilty, but her ministry became more balanced, and Ann was happier. She decided she was not making some kind of compromise when she spent time with people just because she liked them.

New City, New Relationships

Two and a half years ago Ann had to leave the city where she was living. The situation had become unstable, and foreigners were no longer allowed to live there. Her new city, in another part of the country, is more cosmopolitan. The people are less relational. Ann had no choice in the matter; the strategy and her relationships had to change. Now her ministry forces her into contact with people she isn't sure she likes in a culture she finds less appealing. She works with local believers in relationships that are much more business-like than those she had with her Muslim friends: they are colleagues more than friends. It's a bit lonely. Ann is wistful for the old city.

"Before leaving the old city to go on a trip, every time, I had to pack three days in advance. Forget about the last twenty-four hours; your friends just want to be with you, and as close as possible. They want to soak up as much of you as they can. They will come over and stay the night and huddle as close to you as they can and talk. It's like a slumber party!" In her new city, people are busier and receive drop-in guests with more surprise than welcome. The culture is quite different.

Ann does not miss the pressures of possessive relationships, constant drop-in visitors, and "life in the fishbowl" that she faced living enmeshed in a community of Muslims, but on the other hand, those were people she had come to love. "Now I have tons of freedom but I miss the choice opportunities to really go deep."

18 A Troubled Believer

"I thought Monica had the gift of evangelism and had big dreams for her," says Vivian.* "It's a long story," she adds. "Monica came to our door one day and ended up spending several nights," she begins, pouring herself some more tea. When they first met, Vivian had little idea what an intense relationship she and Monica would have.

Monica first heard the gospel when her husband took her from her village to the capital city. There they got to know another local couple who had accepted Christ, and they brought Monica and her husband to church. Monica became a believer. She loved her husband very much, and for a while he was interested in the gospel. But soon he was pulled away by the world. He ended up leaving Monica when she was four months pregnant with their child. Following tradition, the couple was living with his parents. He simply left one day, saying he would come back, and never did. When the word reached them that their son had married another woman, Monica's mother- and father-in-law sent her away.

Further rejection had forced her back home in her parents' village, where Monica tried to share the gospel with her family. They threw her Christian books in the river. "And that's when she came to us," explains Vivian. Monica was looking for Christian fellowship. Someone had given her Vivian's address. "We were glad to meet her and tried to encourage her. We invited her to come back again and participate in the church. But then she left and we didn't see her for a year or so.

"The next time she showed up she looked totally depressed,

---

* For more about Vivian, see chapter 1. Pajamas in Perspective, 7. Why Moms Should Learn the Language, 15. Bringing the Gospel of Peace, 20. Jesus in the Hospital Ward, 23. Available in the Busiest Season, 42. Even a Healthy Marriage . . . , and 53. One-Room Schoolhouse.

dark, and angry. We learned she had actually been living here in our city for quite a while. She was in our neighborhood trying to resolve a lawsuit that was taking her apartment from her." Monica was quite distressed about the situation, which was consuming all her energy and resources. She was also vulnerable. From there, things went from bad to worse.

Virtual Slavery

After losing her apartment Monica moved in with another neighbor. Every morning this woman made Monica rise at 4 a.m. to cook food, then go sell it in the bazaar and bring back all the money. She used Monica like a slave. And now, Monica told Vivian, the woman wanted to get her into prostitution.

"As my husband and I listened to her story we realized we could not let her stay there," says Vivian. "'She'll never let me go!' said Monica, 'If I try to leave, she'll never let me have my things. If I leave, I lose everything!' We did the only thing we could do: we got a truck and our car and several women from the church, went and loaded up all of Monica's things, and brought them here.

"Our intent was that she would stay with us for just two weeks. But as we prayed and the days went by, we could see no option but to keep her."

An Exhausting Ministry

"It was completely exhausting. Her two-year-old was totally untrained, and I already had a toddler in the house. It was a very cold winter, and heating was a problem, so we'd all end up in a few rooms of the house most of the day. The house felt very claustrophobic. As soon as Monica's little boy woke up, he would start screaming. My day would both start and end with that angry, demanding screaming."

But the problems were not only external. Monica had a lot of darkness and hurt inside of her, and it all came out in close quarters. "Eventually it became clear that Monica tended to expect a great deal from people and would pour out her anger on those who were closest to her. Since I was the closest one,

Relationships

she was constantly angry and bitter at me for failing to meet her expectations.

"When she chose truth and went to God, she was a totally different person. She was beautiful, with a lovely smile, and lovely to be around. She led others to Christ. But as soon as she'd slip back into her old lies, it was like night and day," says Vivian, sadly.

Vivian was too experienced to be surprised at such darkness at work in her friend, however. "Monica's mom had been really involved with the spirit world, and all her life had taken her to spiritists. Her mother's current husband was not Monica's father; he didn't want her around. Monica felt nobody wanted her. She must have grown up without love. In reaction, she became a spoiled brat."

This relationship with Monica stimulated Vivian to prepare a study in the local language on healing past wounds and breaking spiritual bondages. Much of her material came from Neil Anderson's book *The Bondage Breaker.* As they worked through the study, Monica and other local believers were able to discover the patterns and wounds that pulled them away from believing the truth and following God. Vivian, too, saw healing and growth in her own life.

Vivian invested in Monica as much as she could. She felt that it was the right thing to do. But she was not at liberty to invest all of her emotional energy into one person. As co-leader of a church-planting team, there were others she had to care for.

"Finally one of our neighbors was going away and needed someone to watch his house for six months, so Monica moved in there. We also arranged for her to be apprenticed to a seamstress in our neighborhood. When the six months were up, she thought she could move back in with us, but we did not make that an option."

While loving freely and sharing hospitality generously are part of Vivian's way of life, they do have limits. Vivian finally felt she had to send Monica back to her village, in spite of her desire to stay in the city. "I just couldn't take it," Vivian says.

19 More Than a Chore

Like many women ministering across Central Asia, Carol has felt the frustration of not knowing how to respond to the practical needs of her friends and neighbors. She wants to be involved in their whole lives and invite them into hers. But it doesn't always—or even often!—go according to plan. Like many a missionary woman in the region, she finds herself taking initiative again and again, reaching out to women who can't seem to make weekly meetings but show up unexpectedly at other times.

The local women carry heavy loads. One traditional proverb has it that women have forty souls—so they always have strength and energy to keep working. In many cases, husbands and mothers-in-law deny them freedom to go places. As in many Muslim cultures, ministry must be carried on in a low-key way. To touch these women, one must come alongside them in practical ways and help them respond to the circumstances and challenges of their lives.

Carol goes to the bazaar with her local friends. Another worker makes jam with neighbors. Some women cook with their local friends. In these ways they can get their work done together. But establishing a consistent relationship with someone who lives on the other side of town is more difficult. During the winter, when the days are short, the weather often keeps people inside. Discipleship seems to shut down. How can you disciple women if you never see them?

Creative Solutions

Peggy comes from a Muslim background, but had been a follower of Christ for several years when Carol met her. In fact, her husband helps lead one of the emerging churches in their city. Carol and Peggy want to spend time together in a discipleship relationship. However, each of them has two small children, and

Relationships

Peggy lives clear on the other side of the city. To meet with Carol, Peggy depends on her husband, who has a car, to remember to drive her to Carol's house and pick her up. It is equally hard for Carol to get to Peggy's house. As a result, their meetings have been frustratingly infrequent.

Or at least they were. Then Carol discovered a practical incentive to help Peggy make their appointments consistently. The answer? The use of her washing machine!

While not unheard of, few women in the city have access to such a timesaving device as a washing machine. Instead they spend hours each week doing their families' laundry by hand. So Peggy comes to Carol's house to use her machine. Now that she has practical help with her home responsibilities, Peggy has found a way to meet with Carol every week. The big load of laundry sitting in their front room may help Peggy's husband remember which day it is as well! Now doing laundry is more than a chore: it's a time for Peggy to grow in her faith.

The use of a washing machine may seem a prosaic motivation for studying the Bible together, but it also gives Carol a way to show Peggy how much she cares for her. In the year and a half since the arrangement began, Carol says, Peggy has become a mighty woman of God. Another practical draw, adds Carol, is to serve Peggy and other guests a nutritious meal. Friends from the villages, especially, can rarely afford to buy meat.

Discipleship

When Peggy and Carol get together, they begin with a bit of worship and singing, then read the Scriptures together, talk about their lives, and spend time in prayer. Praying together has been a challenge for Carol. When she first began she could not pray fluently in the local language, but learning has been well worth it.

"When you pray with people, you are doing two things," explains Carol. "First, of course, you are praying! And that's a good thing in and of itself. Second, you are modeling prayer." She prays with Peggy and other believers about the issues in their lives and uses maps, Scriptures, and other creative ideas to help them keep an outward focus and intercede for others.

Another important aspect of discipleship is just talking about life. But this brings up some challenges. Local believers' lives are so different from Carol's that it's hard for Carol to understand at times. Local women are reluctant to talk about the "old ways" of pleasing the spirits that still control the way Central Asian women live, but these things need to be brought out in the open. Spiritual bondage can be a huge block to the spiritual growth of believers. Little by little, Carol has learned to recognize the signs and results of magic and bondage in the lives of her friends.

At first, Carol prepared book and Bible studies and led Peggy through them. But as the months have gone by, their meetings have taken on a different look. Currently, Peggy is reading the book of John on her own and bringing Carol questions as she has them. The two spend more time in prayer, and they can pray and share more deeply now. Carol sees herself as not discipling a woman, but mentoring a leader who reaches out to others.

Equipping New Leaders

Last summer Carol got a new house helper who was interested in studying the Bible, as well. Jackie's husband would not approve of her going to a Bible study. However, he did not mind if she and Carol developed a relationship and talked about spiritual things when she was at work. So, with Peggy, Jackie, and a few others, Carol began a small-group Bible study. Peggy is now leading these meetings, using basic discipleship materials recently developed by a ministry team in another part of the country. Carol and Peggy both hope these women will be able to go through the same material with others.

Jackie and her sisters have been believers for more than two years now, but their lives have been steeped in folk Islam. It's still difficult for Carol to talk to them about such things, but the women talk to Peggy more freely. She's in a better place to understand. Folk Islam is part of Peggy's background, too.

"If we disciple women here, we must disciple them to disciple others, because they'll be so much more effective than we are," says Carol.

Carol's role now is to help Peggy. She spends time with Peggy before and after the meetings, helping prepare the lessons and praying and talking about their own lives. She also takes care of the women's children while they meet. Things have come a long way. These days, while Peggy leads Bible studies in her house, Carol can usually be found in the kitchen, happily stirring a big pot of soup and keeping all the kids out of trouble. She wouldn't have it any other way.

Peggy doesn't live across town anymore. She recently moved just around the corner from Carol's family. She doesn't need a ride and often comes on her own now, bringing her kids. "And," says Carol, "she doesn't always bring her laundry!"

20 Jesus in the Hospital Ward

Anemia is a common problem in the areas where Vivian* lives, especially among pregnant women. They do not get the iron they need as part of their diet, so they often go to the hospital for a few weeks for treatment and a "rest." The women find it can be a nice break from their hard labor, although there is not much to do there.

One believer, the first in her village to receive Christ, came to Vivian's city to go to the hospital there and be treated for anemia. Janet had become a believer through the ministry of her close relative, Norman, who lived in the city. When Norman visited his sister in the hospital, he brought her a New Testament and other gospel materials to read while she rested. She appreciated his thoughtfulness, and started passing the books around to the other women sharing her room. Vivian was a friend of Janet's as well, so it was only natural for her to visit Janet and bring her meals, not provided in most Central Asian hospitals.

Three Surprising Bribes

"When I went to visit her," says Vivian, "I found these women really interested in what they were reading. As I sat talking about it with Janet I said, 'Wouldn't it be great if they could see the film about Jesus?' The ladies in her room responded, 'Maybe we can! Let's ask the nurse if she'll let us out at night, and we'll come to your house and see it!'"

With some reluctance, the nurse agreed to let the women leave

---

* For more about Vivian, see chapter 1. Pajamas in Perspective, 7. Why Moms Should Learn the Language, 15. Bringing the Gospel of Peace, 18. A Troubled Believer, 23. Available in the Busiest Season, 42. Even a Healthy Marriage . . . , and 53. One-Room Schoolhouse.

Relationships

for an evening, when the doctors were not around. But she wanted a payment for violating hospital policy: "You have to bring me back a plate of the food," she said. Vivian was happy to make one extra share of dinner that night!

Two women came to Vivian's house to see the *Jesus* film. Both were deeply moved. The next day when Vivian went to see them at the hospital, both made a commitment to Christ. Vivian was surprised, and practically tried to talk them out of it. "I told them how many people would be against them. But they insisted they were ready and wanted to receive him!" she says.

Vivian was concerned about how other people would react to their decision and wanted to equip the women to face opposition. She wanted to have them to her house again to talk to them more. "This time when we asked the nurse, she said, 'I'll let you take them out, but only if you give me a copy of the film about Jesus, too!' Vivian was even happier to pay this second bribe than the first.

Some of the anemic women, having completed their treatments, left to go home, but others arrived. After meeting Janet, they too were reading the Bible and wanted to see the film about Jesus. "Maybe we can just ask the nurse if you can bring the movie and show it to us here!" suggested one. This time the nurse agreed, "But you have to give me a copy of the Bible, too!" she added. There was nothing Vivian would rather do.

In God's Hands

"I did not know what to think of this whole situation!" says Vivian. Because of restrictions in her host country, she tried to be careful about openly sharing her faith. "Sharing the gospel almost randomly in a public setting would not have been our strategy! But it really seemed that God was the one opening the doors.

"Here I was, this foreign woman, going to the hospital every other day, and sharing the gospel with women from all over the region who are probably telling their husbands all about me! What would the authorities say if they found out? But I prayed, 'God, this is in your hands; all I know is to continue going as long as I have 'friends' to visit.'"

When the *Jesus* film was shown in the hospital, Janet's believing relative, Norman, came as well. After eight of the women watched the film, he shared his testimony about how he had changed since receiving Christ. "That was sort of the gripping point; all these women wanted their husbands to change and be like Norman!" says Vivian with a laugh. In the years since, she has seen it happen more than once: one of the most attractive things about the gospel, for local women, is how it can change men! The next day, three more women received Christ, bringing the total to seven.

"Still, I wondered, 'God, why are you doing this, drawing to yourself these women who are scattered all over the region and are just going to go home? They will have no fellowship, and their husbands more than likely will oppose their faith. Is this very strategic?'"

Following Up

The only appropriate response was to pray that God would use it. Vivian and her friends tried to send copies of the Bible home with each of the ladies. One of them asked, "Can you write a message to my husband in my Bible?" Vivian had her husband, Trent, write a nice note to the woman's husband and included it in the book, asking for God's blessing on him through the words he would read.

Three months later, young believers attending a ministry-training seminar were given the assignment to track down these anemic women, now scattered to their villages. The believers went to each woman's home to hand deliver invitations from Trent and Vivian to come to their house as guests. Two couples came. One went home early; they may have been more interested in the novelty of knowing foreigners than they were in the faith.

But the woman who had asked for a note to her husband, Bill, came and brought him. As soon as they walked in, Bill said, "Where is this man who wrote the note to me? I want to meet him!" When Vivian's husband came out, Bill gave Trent a big hug. The two ended up staying the night, and watching the *Jesus* film together again.

Relationships

"As we watched the *Jesus* film, he kept saying, 'Oh, now he's going to do this . . . here's what he's going to say next.' This man amazed us. Bill was just a village truck driver, but he had read the Bible we sent home with his wife and remembered everything in it!"

Bill decided to follow Jesus, and he was not going to turn back. He began instructing his whole family to walk in "the Way" and was not concerned by neighbors or relatives' opinions. "He was a wonderful, warm, open guy," says Vivian. "He was a great man with lots of potential as a leader, not just in his own village but also beyond."

One sour note in this encouraging story is that before long, Bill started complaining of stomach pains. By the time they discovered his cancer, it had spread throughout his body and he soon died. "He had so much potential!" Vivian says. Before he died, though, he instructed his believing wife to raise their children in "the Way"—something she has done. Vivian would not have thought this little ministry in a hospital ward would bear such fruit.

21 A Ministry in Baby Season

"My ministry has ebbed and flowed with the seasons in life," explains Sally.* A missionary for twenty years or more, Sally and her husband Jim have lived in several parts of the Muslim world and raised a large family. Now some of her kids are in their teens. But when Sally and her family lived in the Middle East, there were times when she was "just having babies," as she puts it. "I couldn't be out sitting and talking with my neighbors as much as I wanted because of the kids. Besides, my language was not really good enough!"

Like many women making the transition from a career—of any kind—to motherhood, Sally felt frustrated. She felt like a failure. Her husband tried to reassure her. "I need you in the home and supporting me. It's okay you aren't spending a lot of time with the neighbors," he said. "It's just a season. Give yourself permission for it to be different."

Sally has always been one of those women who knew she couldn't be happy as the "accompanying spouse," letting her husband carry on the ministry while she managed the home—but she also knew she might spend many years homeschooling her children, which she did. She loved the ministry of homeschooling. But she had to accept that she might not be able to have the kind of ministry outside the home that she wanted. Sally had also been reluctant to participate very much in the active expatriate community in their Middle Eastern city. After all, wouldn't that take her away from "real ministry"? What kind of work might God have for her during this "baby season"?

---

* For more about Sally, see chapter 24. Does God Want Us Overseas? and 34. "To Know God and Know Myself."

Relationships

A Ministry to Moms

To Sally's surprise, she ended up ministering to other missionaries. "Many of them were just there for language school, preparing to head into frontier situations. They were young and inexperienced. By helping them just get a hold of life and be mentored as mothers, I could make a kingdom impact," she explains. As these young women spent time in Sally's home and saw how she managed her house and children, her devotional life, and commitment to family—along with the demands of ministry and living cross-culturally—those Sally mentored were equipped to say, "I know what it will take. I know it can be done."

Some of the tricks and tips the women learned from Sally were quite simple and practical. Take kitchen timers, for example. "I use my kitchen timers for everything!" explains Sally. In fact, as her family has recently relocated to a new country, Sally is on the lookout for a good place to replenish her supply. "Kitchen timers are great for keeping track of how long the kids have been doing things—whether that's playing, drawing, doing drills on the computer, or working on their math or reading. Frankly, I can't keep track of it all because I have so many kids." Sally's sons and daughters can set the timers themselves; it saves her work and makes everything fair. "People tell me, 'I never would have thought of that!' But I can't live without my kitchen timers!"

Keep It in Perspective

"When you go through a season when you can't do much 'ministry,' it's easy to start comparing yourself to others. You say, 'I'm not as useful as so-and-so in Pakistan!'" says Sally. She is still as busy with her kids as she was with her babies, but Sally treasures the way God has used her gifts and limitations in this season. She's also grateful for the encouragement she received from her husband to embrace what God had for her at different stages of life. "When you are struggling with your role," she says, "you need someone who can say, 'Quit beating yourself over the head. This is what you're supposed to be doing!'"

Discussion Questions for Part 2

Chapter 12: God Gives Us Influence

1. If you have been in ministry as a single person and as a married person, how has your life and ministry changed, and how have you responded?

2. Has the Lord opened up surprising avenues for you in new situations?

Chapter 13: Loving Muslims in Her Own Country

1. In what ways have you seen a community differently as an insider than as an outsider? What helps someone become an insider?

2. Joyce mentioned crying and praying with her Muslim friends. Can you think of other things that would express love and compassion in your host culture?

Chapter 14: A Place for Broken People

1. Share a story about how God broke you and used your brokenness to help other people. What difficult things in your life has he healed and/or redeemed?

2. What are the challenges facing the people you minister to? How might you respond to them with identification and compassion?

3. What stories about the things God has done most give you hope? How have you seen him at work in the lives of women you know?

Chapter 15: Bringing the Gospel of Peace

1. What needs do hurting people in your host culture express? What deeper needs seem to be behind them?

2. What good news does Jesus offer them?

3. Are there things local believers can say and do that foreigners can't? What about vice versa? What are ways to work together?

4. What do you think about celebrating Christian holidays with Muslim friends and neighbors?

Chapter 16: An Abundance of Friendships

1. Do you have a local best friend? How has this relationship helped you adjust? If you don't have one, share how the others can pray for you in this.

2. How might you build a broad base of relationships?

3. If your base is already too broad, what are some culturally appropriate ways you might invest more deliberately in fewer friends?

Chapter 17: Choosing Your Friendships

1. What do people expect from a friend in your host culture? To what extent are you able or willing to meet their expectations?

2. In what ways are your ideas about friendship different from your host culture's ideas? How do both compare to biblical models?

3. What lessons have you learned from people you've been close to who see things differently than you do?

Chapter 18: A Troubled Believer

1. Have you ever decided to invest in a relationship and then seen it take over your life like Vivian did?

2. Would you be willing to have a troubled local believer live in your home? Why or why not? What do you think you might expect?

3. Discuss your philosophy of spiritual oppression. What have your experiences been?

4. What formative influences have left women in your ministry scarred and in bondage? What can you do to help them recognize and overcome these influences?

Chapter 19: More Than a Chore

1. What things might limit local women's availability and willingness to spend time with you?

2. What are some practical ways you could come alongside local women for the sake of relationship building?

3. What might it look like to disciple a local woman in your context?

4. Have you seen local women become equipped to disciple others? What kind of support do they require?

Chapter 20: Jesus in the Hospital Ward

1. Could you share the gospel as openly as Vivian did? Would you have the same concerns if you did?

2. What do you think about Vivian's concern that reaching sick and scattered women doesn't seem "strategic," and her willingness to reach them anyway?

3. Discuss some of the ways you have seen believers, especially those who seem to have a lot of ministry potential like Bill, "taken out of the picture"? What helps you persevere when you see setbacks like that?

Chapter 21: A Ministry in Baby Season

1. What have been the main seasons of your life? How have they been different from one another?

2. What limits your ministry? How are you responding?

3. What practical tips have helped you manage your life?

4. Is there someone to whom you can pass on what has worked for you?

Part 3:
Life under Pressure

Staying Anchored during Storms

22 The Cost of Compassion

Soon after Jennifer* became a Christian, God called her to be a missionary. She was already studying to be a nurse and was eager to develop a ministry of compassion as the Lord worked through both her skills and her prayers. When she and her family first began their ministry in Central Asia, Jennifer wanted to help everyone. Isn't that what Jesus would do?

"We wanted to sow seeds broadly. Anyone who came along with a need could be someone whose heart God was going to soften. How could I turn them away? If they were sick, I could help with diagnosis, sometimes. Always I could lay hands on them and pray for a miracle, which, a lot of times, was what they needed!"

A Medical Ministry Gets Out of Control

Families in the impoverished neighborhood where Jennifer, Robert, and their children live started to come to the foreign nurse with their medical problems. "Some of them were coming to me for every little thing," says Jennifer. It wasn't long before she found herself in over her head, both with the frequency of the requests and the seriousness of some of their illnesses.

One neighbor had a ten-year-old daughter whose diabetes was raging out of control. Jennifer prayed for the girl and talked to the strong Muslim family about Jesus and his desire to heal their daughter. There was little else she could do, and that was hard for both Jennifer and the neighbor family to accept. "Wanting to see this girl well weighed on me so much! Eventually—this is so

---

* For more about Jennifer, see chapter 16. An Abundance of Friendships, 30. Suddenly Rich, and 50. The Perils of Parenting Preschoolers.

sad!—we were out of town, and when we came back the little girl was dead," says Jennifer.

"Eventually I discovered it was too much for me to try to help everyone," says Jennifer. By this time a few years had passed and the young church her team was working with had begun to grow. Jennifer decided to limit her medical ministry to nursing believers. "Then one year all the believers were sick all winter. They came to me at all hours of the night! We had all these medications we had brought over, and we wanted to use them, so we basically became the church's pharmacy."

Jennifer was still trying to save everyone. She saw the weaknesses of the local medical system and felt terrible about sending her friends to "bad doctors" and treatments that wouldn't help or were not needed. "With my experience and knowledge, I wanted to make sure they got the help they did need. A lot of it was beyond me, but as a compassionate person I wanted to look in every single book, get on the Internet, and call a bunch of doctors to try to figure out what it might be."

Jennifer had to learn that she could not fix every problem. "One of my huge lifestyle changes was learning to say, 'I'm a nurse, not a doctor. You need to go see a doctor. I can't help you.'" Jennifer still does nursing, like checking blood pressure and treating colds and using her medical books, but she doesn't tackle doctor things like diabetes or cancer.

She also learned that the problem was bigger than her amount of energy and experience; she was creating dependency and needed to stop for the good of those to whom she was ministering. The church and neighborhood had become dependent on her, and they had also picked up her negative views on the local medical system. But now that has changed. "I've gotten to the point where I can release them to the doctor. When I send them to a doctor, we both know they may not get the help they need. But we pray together, asking God to lead them to good doctors and to give the doctors wisdom."

Life under Pressure ❁

Chronic Fatigue Syndrome

After years of sowing broadly, showing compassion generously, and pouring her life into her live-in disciples, Jennifer's health began to decline. She had what was eventually diagnosed as chronic fatigue syndrome (CFS) along with a host of related immune-system ailments. CFS is still something of a mystery to doctors, and causes and treatment plans vary. CFS sufferers may feel or be told that they are "making up" the aches, pains, and weariness that come to characterize their lives and interfere with their daily activities.

"I really fought the CFS. I didn't want to 'receive' that I could have it! I am naturally a high-energy person; how could I be chronically tired? It was terrible! I was just so tired and had no energy for anything. At first I did not have the energy to make a meal. Then later I didn't even have the energy just to do the dishes afterwards. Finally, when I didn't have the energy to pull the meat of the bone, I knew it was time to go home."

Following an unscheduled furlough so Jennifer could be treated for CFS, she and Robert returned to the field. This time, though, they made a list of changes for the way they lived and began to put these changes into practice.

One of the first things they did was to find a good house helper. They also started taking more regular breaks outside their city and decided not to have guests live with them for more than two weeks at a time. And, in spite of the ambiguous demands of the local culture—you never know who will come to your house and when—they found ways to stick to a weekly schedule including time to focus on God, their marriage and family, work, and rest.

The biggest change, though, may have been what Robert and Jennifer call "the humble recognition that we can't meet everyone's needs!"

"There are certain good works that God has prepared for us beforehand, and we must do them. If we're spending our time and energy doing other 'good' things he hasn't meant for us, it will take away from the best and still not really meet those other needs either. We must trust in God to take care of everyone's needs, not us!

"I have to humbly admit I can't save the world and protect the people I love," says Jennifer. "This was a huge reality check for me, and it required a major life change."

Healing through Prayer

People still come to Jennifer for medical help, and often she can't help them. But the Lord has used Jennifer's prayers to heal and stir up the faith of many. "How freeing it is, now, to be able to say, 'I don't know what you have. But Jesus can help you.'

"Praying for people in time of need is one of the most powerful and easiest things to do. Everyone has a need. Pray for them all, even if you can't help them. Prayer answers everything. There's no limit to what prayer can do! So, let's pray! When I have asked people if I can pray for them, I've never had anyone say no."

23

Available in the Busiest Season

Being available or abandoned to God's will, rather than protective about her own time and space, has been one of the best ways Vivian* has found to secure contentment in ministry and motherhood. While there is a time for saying no, Vivian explains, "It's too stressful to live protectively. When I can make myself come to a place of saying, 'Okay, Lord, I am here for you,' it turns out to be much more pleasant and fruitful."

Life in the Busy Season

Around her fourth year on the field, when things were at their busiest, Vivian counted how many guests she fed and entertained during a three-week period. The figures were above 150. "When we averaged it out, we realized we had people spending the night five nights out of seven. These were not people we had invited or planned on; almost all of them were drop-ins!" Sometimes Vivian would cook, serve, and clean up after guests three times a day before falling into bed exhausted.

Today her kids are older and well adjusted. They are helpful around the house and often answer the door and phone. In those days she had to do it all herself. With the children's frequent problems with diarrhea and illness, Vivian had to balance serving, cooking, and answering the door with frequent emergency breaks to get her kids to the toilet. "It was a very busy time of life. I knew it was not always going to be this way. I was a mother of three young children, all under four years old."

In addition, a local man who was the first believer in the area

---

* For more about Vivian, see chapter 1. Pajamas in Perspective, 7. Why Moms Should Learn the Language, 15. Bringing the Gospel of Peace, 18. A Troubled Believer, 20. Jesus in the Hospital Ward, 42. Even a Healthy Marriage . . . , and 53. One-Room Schoolhouse.

was starting to see his ministry and relationships take off. And he was living at Trent and Vivian's house. While he was a great help and blessing, she was also entertaining his guests as well as her own.

Time to set boundaries, you might think. But Vivian disagrees. She says she and her husband would lie in bed and think about it. "'Wow, we had a lot of people today!' If we looked ahead and said, 'Tomorrow are we going to have a day like this? Oh no!' We'd think it over, though, and say, 'They were all really fruitful, great times. May the Lord continue to use us and our house this way.' We weren't planning the crazy schedule. It was just happening."

When You Can't Pace Your Life

"We would say, 'We need to pace our lives,' then wonder, 'How?' We couldn't figure out how to do it. In this culture, you just don't send anyone away when they come to your door, especially if they come from far away! So when, at two or three in the morning, we would have people coming in from the capital and knocking on our door; we'd get up, get everything out, feed them, and take care of them."

Teammates living in an apartment in another part of the city would sometimes lock their door, and turn off the lights, and sit in their central room by candlelight, not answering the door or the phone. That way they could have a "date night" in the dark and quiet. But Vivian and her family could not pretend not to be home. The neighbors could tell.

Others in their region planned regular getaways to another city, usually the capital. But for Trent and Vivian, finding a place with space and quiet and nobody who wanted to talk to them was challenging. "We'd be traveling with babies, too. The capital was even more a Russian-language setting then than it is now; so people would be yelling at us for not speaking Russian. It didn't feel like a good place to get away.

"Sometimes I'd think, 'Tonight, or tomorrow, I'm just going to have a day of rest, a quiet day. I'm going to catch up. Or, I'll just do some family stuff, bake something nice for my family,

Life under Pressure ❧

or work on my photos.' There was always one thing or another that I was dreaming about. I'd have this dream and my list, and every day it wouldn't work. The doorbell would ring, and inside I'd tighten up and start thinking, 'How can I send them away?' I'd walk out to the gate kind of disgruntled and welcome them in because I had to."

An Attitude of Availability

It wasn't long before Vivian realized this was not a healthy way to live. The problem was not having too many guests or having the wrong things on her list as much as it was that she had expectations that could not be met. "It's so stressful to live like that, and it wears me out.

"God just spoke to my heart and showed me the need every day to just offer my list to him, saying, 'If this is what you want me to get done today, great. If you bring someone else, I want to trust that you brought them.' Every time the phone rang or there was a knock at the door, I would say, 'Here I am, Lord, I'm your handmaid.' I'd say that inside, and go. It so changed me on those days. It liberated me to go with the flow and be more like Jesus. Jesus wasn't upset and frustrated that people were crowding in and changing his plans!

"Availability, seeing 'interruptions' as God's opportunities, is a much less stressful way to handle a busy life. I do feel we were stretched beyond what we thought we could handle. The pace went on and on and on. But if we had tried to stick to our own schedule and protect our lives and all that, we really would have burned out."

Following a Central Asian Lifestyle

Living according to the local style also relieved a lot of Vivian's stress and anxiety. Local food requires a few simple ingredients that are always on hand, and entertaining guests overnight requires only stacks of quilts and big open rooms. Living this way as much as possible made it easier for Vivian to respond graciously when guests came. Figuring out how to cook Western food and set up a Western household would be a huge challenge. Learning to cook local food and enjoy local ways of life was much less stressful. "Everything you need is available. Besides, when you ask your local friends to teach you how to cook, you get to know them and practice the local language," says Vivian.

Occasionally, however, she would want to do something "American" with her kids, like making a meal from ingredients she wouldn't serve to local guests. Sometimes it was just on the spur of a moment. "We don't have anything planned, let's do something special!" Vivian would tell her kids. Eventually she started trying to spread the word that Fridays were their "family night." But even then she had to hold her plans with open hands. As soon as the lasagna came out of the oven, a whole family of local guests, who did not know what to think of such strange food, might arrive.

Your Attitude, Your Kids' Attitude

"If someone comes on 'family night,' I have to give it to the Lord and help the kids say, 'God brought him over. There must be a reason. We'll have family night another night.' When people show up, I can't mutter to my kids, 'I wish they hadn't come!'" Vivian has found that whatever her attitude may be, her children's attitude will probably be the same.

Encouraging her children to participate in the ministry is a big part of helping them value the local culture. Since women's ministry, especially, is largely home-based in Vivian's host culture, that means helping them to enjoy offering hospitality. Vivian's children play "guest, guest" with their friends on the street, setting up pretend houses and inviting each other over for "meals." When their parents' guests come, Trent and Vivian's kids help set the table and get out the little dishes of nuts, raisins, and candy. If they can enjoy offering hospitality and see their mother doing the same, they won't see guests as something that takes their parents away from them.

For Vivian, an important part of raising her kids overseas is to help them love and be happy in both cultures. She and her husband avoid criticizing the local culture in front of them and help them to look for and find the things they will like and value. At the same time, they try not to put down their home culture in front of them either. Vivian's hope is that her kids will grow up appreciating both cultures. They, too, need to learn to be available to God.

24 Does God Want Us Overseas?

"Our oldest daughter is in heaven," says Sally.* Sally and her husband Jim have lived in several parts of the Muslim world in the last several decades, and each transition has brought its own challenges. But one of the toughest times came when their six-year-old daughter, Katie, died of leukemia, and during that time of illness they had to go back to the States. During Katie's illness, Sally learned about God's sovereignty. "I had to! Do we pray for God to heal her, or pray for her to die and be out of pain?

"Unfortunately, the worst wounds we got during this time were from the church. People would say, 'If you had enough faith, your daughter would be healed.' That had the opposite effect of what they intended. Instead of looking to God, it put our eyes on ourselves, trying to drum up faith."

Overwhelming Debt

Losing their little girl was a wrenching time for Sally and her husband, but it also strained them financially. By the time their daughter died, they owed $60,000 in medical debt. Back in their home country for a season, Jim was either unemployed or underemployed. How could they pay off such a debt, and how long would it take?

The burden of this debt may have tested their faith as much as the loss of their precious daughter. "We felt so strongly that God wanted us back overseas! We were even willing to take our daughter when she was still sick with leukemia, if he opened the door for us. With so many not willing to go, here we were ready and willing!" Yet how could they go back overseas with such

---

* For more about Sally, see chapter 21. A Ministry in Baby Season and 34. To Know God and Know Myself.

114 Life under Pressure

a burden of debt? They sought the counsel of godly, ministry-minded friends who agreed that God wanted them overseas. But under the circumstances, how could it happen?

"The hospital and oncologist knew us. They had seen the integrity of our family for two and a half years. Our daughter was a beautiful little girl. I know that's a mother's point of view, but she was! She made friends with anyone who walked by her room, including Sister Virginia, who was the head of the hospital. She would come read stories aloud to our little girl."

After Katie died, news of the family's debt reached Sister Virginia. She came to Sally and her husband and said, "One of the purposes of a Catholic hospital is to exercise charity where it's needed."

"Then she forgave us our debt!" Eight weeks after they lost their little girl in her battle against cancer, Sally's family was debt-free. When the doors finally opened, they were able to go back overseas.

"Sometimes now, years later, I get tense about money," admits Sally, "but then I have to say to myself, 'Where is your brain? Don't you have a memory? Don't you remember what God did?'"

Dealing with an Uncertain Future

The trial over Katie's leukemia was not the last for Sally's family. Over the years they have faced several more of those unforeseen events that force ministry families back home for a time. Sally found it hard to see these as more than temporary interruptions. "The last time we were in the States I didn't unpack, emotionally, for several months," says Sally. "I was so sure we wouldn't stay. Both my oldest daughter and I had terrible reverse culture stress!" Again, they were walking in ambiguity. Would they return to the country in which they had been living? If not, where would they go next?

"We had left our home overseas in a hurry. Later my husband and I had to go back, without the kids, and pack up the house by ourselves—even the kids' rooms. It was terrible. We'd find a rock in the closet and say, 'Is this from the beach on the day one of the kids was baptized, or is it just any old rock that we can throw away?'"

Even during this difficult time, God gave the family the encouragement they needed to keep pursuing cross-cultural ministry. As Sally and her husband flew back to North America after packing all their belongings, they had a long layover in Amsterdam, one of Europe's most international cities. "As we walked around the airport, we heard people speaking Turkish, Arabic, and Spanish. We felt our spirits lift. We love living in other cultures. Maybe there's a gift for living cross-culturally. If so, does it make sense for us to be at home?"

When challenges like sickness and finances threaten to keep kingdom workers off the field, many find strength in a sense of personal calling. Sally finds her sense of calling simply in the Word of God. "As far as I'm concerned, the call is in the Book! What else do I need? The command is to go; from our perspective you have to have a call to stay." At any rate, she says, for her family, "Doing kingdom work is our natural environment.

"As Dawson Trotman, the founder of The Navigators, said, 'Never do things others can do and will do if there are things others cannot do or will not do.'"

25 Commitment under Crisis

Ginny, her husband Jack, and their two children live in a small city in a volatile part of South Asia where personal safety cannot be taken for granted. When crises came, however, Ginny* experienced unexpected measures of God's grace.

It had been a hectic season. Her oldest son had just turned three, and now they had a baby. Their landlord had decided to stop renting to them, so they had moved to a new place down the street. "We hadn't even unpacked, but we had to make a 'visa run' to the capital. 'We'll be back in two weeks,' I thought, 'then we'll really move in, and start living happily ever after.'"

While in the capital, Ginny and her family visited an international church located in a diplomatic enclave. It was supposed to be a safe area. The first time they went, armed guards surrounded the church. The second time they were a little puzzled to see no guards.

After taking Liam, their older son, to the nursery, Ginny settled back to listen to the sermon. "The baby fell asleep in my lap. I kicked off my shoes and crossed my legs. It was a hot spring morning, and the sermon was kind of boring. My mind began to wander . . ."

The sudden sound of something like fireworks in the back of the church attracted Ginny's attention. Was it a joke? A skit? "I turned around and saw the commotion; people in the back row were getting up in a panic. I saw and started to smell smoke, and there were pieces of debris in the air. Then I realized, 'Somebody is shooting at us. This could be the last moment of my life.'"

---

* For more about Ginny, see chapter 5. Those Who Persevere and 31. Life in Seclusion.

Getting Out

"I wasn't panicking. I felt like I was packed in cotton, and that everything was moving in slow motion. My two thoughts were for God and my husband, my two most important relationships. Am I all right with God?" She knew she was. "I was so glad; you know if he takes you, you go to a good place. So the next thing I wanted to be sure of was that I was right with Jack.

"Pieces of debris were flying through the air. The moment I started looking around for a way to get out, Jack grabbed me. He pushed me down and threw himself on top of us. The baby woke as I hit the floor, and a bomb went off. That bomb perforated my ears, but not the baby's. Because he was crying, he had no pressure in his ears! As we tried to get out, I was still barefoot and carrying the baby. My only thoughts were, 'Don't step on the glass and get out.' I felt weaker and weaker, looked down, and saw there was blood all down my left side. 'Oh my God,' I thought, 'I've been hit!'

"We had just finished a Muslim holiday when they slaughter animals in sacrifice rituals. We had been seeing a lot of intestines and inner parts of animals laying in the gutters. As we made it to the foyer I saw something like that and vaguely realized it was from a human being. But because I was looking down and focusing on not stepping on glass, I didn't actually see anyone lying on the ground dead or wounded. Isn't that just God's mercy?

"A friend came up to us holding our older son and said, 'I have him; he's okay! I'll take care of him.' What a relief, that someone we know was taking care of our son."

Once outside, Jack and Ginny saw a family they knew. The wife was wounded, but the husband was not, and his car was parked in front of the church. Moreover, he knew the best hospital to go to and took Jack and Ginny along. Ginny's wounds were significant. "As we were driving to the hospital, I was thinking, 'This takes so long; we're never getting there!'"

Even as a three-year-old, Liam seemed to know what had happened. "He kept saying, 'Those bad men, they did it on purpose!' I was so surprised that he understood," says Ginny.

Life under Pressure

Ginny's arm, the one that had been holding her baby, was shattered, along with her eardrum. She went into surgery. She and her family stayed at the hospital in the capital for a few days and then were evacuated to Ginny's home country in Europe. Insurance provided a nurse to fly with the family and take care of Ginny. The nurse ended up minding the children more than Ginny, but that's what Ginny needed most.

When the family arrived in Europe, it was morning, and that evening Ginny was in surgery again. This time she stayed in the hospital for ten days. Jack and Ginny were blessed with the opportunity to stay in Ginny's home country for several months of physical therapy, after which they returned to South Asia. Ginny's parents, not believers, had a hard time saying goodbye. They were dismayed that she would go back to the place where she had suffered and where she would not be able to get much medical care. They accepted her conviction that she needed to return, though. Friends and neighbors in their Muslim city had also been greatly worried. They were surprised but delighted at Jack and Ginny's courage and commitment to come back, even after what had happened to them.

A New Appreciation for Life and Each Other

While nobody would choose to experience a terrorist attack, Ginny says the few months after it happened were a wonderful time for her. "You knew, overwhelmingly, that God protected you and he was right there with you. You may only have a few moments like that in your life."

She is also amazed by how much worse things could have been. Several of the grenades did not go off, for example. "Only four people were killed in that attack. Two were local believers, and two were part of the embassy community. None of the missionaries were killed or sustained major injuries. A lot of the people in that church were being prayed for on a regular basis. People prayed for their protection. It helped.

"Encourage people to pray for missionaries. It might be a matter of life and death. After the attack, I kept saying, 'You can live pretty cheaply in a third-world country, you don't need a lot of money. But you can't live, you can't even survive, without prayer support.'"

This experience has taught Ginny some lessons about gratitude and the preciousness of life. "With my arm, for example, I never thought, 'I have this arm!' Then it was shattered in the bombing. I think differently; I don't take it for granted. Before I thought, 'I have a good husband and nice kids; I love them,' but when you realize that your family can be taken from you in an instant, it gives you a deeper appreciation for them."

Ginny still gets irritated at her husband, children, or teammates for time to time, but she looks at them as gifts that could have been taken from her. "There are still things that drive you bananas, but that's not where the rubber hits the road. So, Jack won't take out the dirty diapers every time I ask him. Yes, it still bugs me! But going through all we have gone through opens up a new inner reality. In a crisis situation, what a person is made of all comes out.

"He jumped on top of me when the bombs hit."

26   Sickness

Dan, Catherine, and their three children had been part of a church-planting and development team in Central Asia for several years when Catherine's health began to deteriorate.* Although she is trained as a nurse and Dan as a doctor, for about six months they had no idea what the problem might be. A racing heart, constant tiredness, and trouble breathing made her think she was having panic attacks. But what about the chronic sinus infections? Plus she had aching muscles and joints and a cough that wouldn't go away. Then came a few symptoms that were even stranger.

"I was sensitive to smells. I couldn't use public transportation; by the time I got where I was going, I'd feel so bad from the smell of gas that I'd have to turn around and come back. It got to the point that if someone was cracking peanuts, the smell would make my chest start hurting."

Even though Catherine took naps during the day, she was hardly able to get up in the morning. A local girl living with the family did most of the cooking and took care of the baby, which helped.

"I couldn't concentrate; I couldn't think! I had major brain fatigue. Not only was I unable to study language, but my short-term memory was terrible; I couldn't even remember what I was doing!" Although mysterious stress-related illnesses like Chronic Fatigue Syndrome seem to be disproportionately common in the mission community, Catherine did not know if she had that condition or anything else one could put a name on. She felt alone. "I felt like I was losing it. I wondered if it was something spiritual."

---

* For more about Catherine, see chapter 37. An Answer to My Prayers, 39. Help with House Help, 47. Helping Your Kids Feel Heard, and 53. One-Room Schoolhouse.

Effect on Others

"Of course this affected other people. I was just barely surviving, draining my family, and struggling with guilt: I didn't want the team always worrying and praying for me and wondering what I was doing on the field." Catherine was also somewhat dismayed at how easily her kids seemed to adjust; they knew Mommy was always resting. "To some extent, the whole family learned to function without me.

"It certainly affected how Dan and I related to one another as a couple. When I was feeling bad, I would not give him any positive feedback or even a smile. He's the only one I felt comfortable venting with, letting him see how bad I felt. So when he came home, often I'd be frowning, or in bed. I just wanted him to take the kids away from me! I told him it wasn't him, that I wasn't rejecting him. He wanted to believe me, but he didn't always."

Catherine discovered that if she let her illness make her depressed or irritable, others would eventually begin to think of her as a depressed and irritable person; they couldn't help it. "Sometimes Dan wondered if my staying in bed was an excuse to get out of things." It was hard for Catherine to explain. "Since I wasn't thinking very well, I often couldn't express what I was thinking or how I felt. What little energy I had, I was expending on guests and visitors. I didn't have anything left for my husband and children.

"One time we went to the capital for a conference, and I got really sick. My heart was racing, and I had diarrhea; I could barely get to the bathroom. It affected my mind too. I thought I was going to die. I was afraid for the kids, too, wondering if they would survive the day. Jacob was a baby, and the girls must have been three and five. Since I thought I was dying, I actually wrote a letter to everyone telling them how much I loved them. It was not much longer after that that we left the field and went home." The family decided they had to go back to America, their home country.

Resting and Recovering at Home

Catherine has mixed feelings about the six months she spent in America. A friend met the family at the airport, which was good: Dan and Catherine weren't sure they could have managed otherwise, with all the kids and luggage. Someone had suggested a residential counseling center for missionaries as a good place to start. It seemed like a good idea, so that's where they went.

While being in an isolated, protected environment is just what some field workers need, it was not the best situation for Dan and Catherine. They didn't have the support system they would have had if they had gone to stay with one of their families, and they didn't have childcare during the day when they had to be in counseling sessions.

"It didn't turn out to be restful at all. I was sick; taking care of my family and going to all the counseling stuff was too much. What we needed was medical care and a support network.

"After we'd been there three weeks, we got the news my dad had died. If we hadn't gone to the counseling center we could have been there to see him. He had a heart attack or something. He was not in great health, but he wasn't expected to die! One day he was out in the garden picking tomatoes, and the next day he died."

Catherine and her family had to scramble to get tickets to go home for the funeral, but it would not have been possible at all had they still been in Central Asia. In spite of their disappointment about not being able to say goodbye to her dad before his death, Dan and Catherine were grateful for the chance to spend time with her mom and family.

The coming months with family and supporting churches proved to be much more restful than their time at the counseling center. A friend from church offered them a house in which to stay. "'Please don't ask us to speak at every Sunday school class; we just want to be part of the church!' we said," explains Catherine. "We got a good counselor there and did some marriage counseling, but we mostly did medical stuff."

Treatment

So what was actually going on in Catherine's body? While they were in America, Catherine had all kinds of tests done, took different kinds of medicine for panic attacks, had her thyroid checked, had her sinuses X-rayed, and went through counseling to see what might be behind her many illnesses.

"It wasn't until we had been through all kinds of medical tests that Dan found a book about food allergies. We were desperate. For the month of December—so, over Christmas, and in America!—I went on a restricted diet: no flour, eggs, milk, or sugar, and not much fruit. As I added things in, I'd sense a reaction and could see what the problems were. I started feeling better almost immediately after I came off all those foods."

Although Catherine's health improved significantly while she was in America, she did not get really effective treatment for her root problems until after her return to Central Asia. What seemed to be behind her conditions was a problem with yeast. Dan and Catherine have come to believe that intolerance to yeast is behind many food allergies and most sinus infections. American doctors are reluctant to provide the kind of treatment they felt Catherine needed.

"The medication I used is only recommended for a few days in the States," she explains. "For it to really do any good, though, you need it for two weeks. I took it for three! We were so disgruntled with the Western medical system, we were willing to try anything. I haven't had one sinus infection since then, and after that I could start eating different kinds of food. It was still a process; I did not recover immediately." Her diet was still restricted. Catherine could eat rice, but no bread or eggs. The first year was difficult. "I was still finding out how much I could tolerate and was relapsing. Plus I felt grumpy about not being able to eat the things I couldn't eat."

Depending on God

Catherine was still in America and starting to feel better when God spoke to her and Dan through a sermon about how God uses

Life under Pressure

weak people. Being sick had really brought 2 Corinthians 12:9 to life for Catherine: "But he said to me, 'My grace is sufficient for you, for my power is made perfect in weakness.' Therefore I will boast all the more gladly about my weaknesses, so that Christ's power may rest on me.

"We made plans to return to the field; Dan and I both really wanted to go back, and the kids did too. I wasn't better yet, but God seemed to be pushing us in that direction. So we made plans to go back. By the time we actually left, I was a lot better: I was almost feeling normal! That was confirmation.

"I had to come to terms with the fact that I couldn't do everything. God taught me through my sickness that he didn't want me to do everything. Maybe it was even his way of discipling me to be more dependent on him for each day.

"That's a big lesson I'm still trying to learn. Even this week, my prayer request to the team is from 1 Peter 4:11, to serve with the strength God provides, not out of my own strength. The principle is that God often uses you when you feel weak, if you let him."

Dan and Catherine didn't learn this lesson alone. Their experience stretched their team's view of sickness and health as well. It turned their thinking around. While still intent on seeking out the best for each person and the team as a whole, the team no longer considers peak health a basic requirement for team members.

27   A Fast Track to Sanctification

Jason and Lisa had some wild years in college before they got married. Although both of them were believers, they had not been walking with the Lord. "So I said," Lisa explains, "'I've been so bad; from here on out whatever God says, I will do. I don't care what it is.'" Jason made the same commitment. After they got married, they told God they wanted to live for him and go wherever he sent them. What God wanted turned out to be more than they had bargained for.

Off to the Hardest Places

"Soon after we got married we met a missionary couple who influenced us. We didn't have a career path, so we said 'We want to be radical for Jesus, so we'll be missionaries!' We both did graduate work to prepare ourselves and joined a team in South Asia."

When Jason got a research grant that took them into an area of their country other workers couldn't get into, the two found themselves without a team. But it seemed worth having the experience of being on the cutting edge of ministry in the Muslim world, living at what seemed the very ends of the earth in connection with members of an unreached people group quite cut off from the outside world. "It was an incredible experience; we were visiting homes every day. I could be closely connected to these women that nobody else could get to! It was a great cross-cultural experience for us; it was wonderful. While we were there we had two little kids, so my language was not coming along very quickly. But somehow we managed to develop deep relationships anyway."

On a visit to their home country, Lisa was still amazed at the experiences she had had. She took a seminary class called

Life under Pressure

Ministering to Muslim Women, which her teacher explained usually meant going to their homes, drinking tea with them, and talking about their marriages and children. "I thought, 'Wow, that's ministry to Muslim women? I have been ministering to Muslim women!' I thought it had to be harder than that!'"

Although the opportunity to build relationships with Muslim women was exciting, the context was full of challenges, and eventually these wore Lisa down. Because it was a very conservative Muslim community, she couldn't leave her house freely and had to wear a veil most of the time. "Plus," she says, "we lived in a two-room house: we were really trying to live like the people. But you really can't live like the people in this country. Sure, we were agonizing over every penny, but our neighbors didn't even have electricity or water."

One time, when their daughter Emma was about one year old, Lisa and Jason visited some friends. They only intended to stay for a short time but had to spend the night when their hosts refused them permission to leave. In a society where being a host is a great honor, guests receive great service but little freedom. This can be hard for a westerner to accept.

"Emma had diarrhea and was throwing up, and we didn't have diapers with us. I am diabetic and didn't have stuff with me. It was a horrible experience!" Things got worse. "Then a man walked in when I was sitting with the women and didn't have my veil on. The mother-in-law threw my veil at me and called me all kinds of names for not having it on!" No matter how hard she tried, Lisa could not measure up to local expectations and was not always sure she wanted to. "All the shame and blame of being a woman there can really wear you down."

Breakdown

What went first was Lisa's health. "I got really sick, and I almost died," says Lisa. She had viral encephalitis, an inflammation of the brain that can lead to severe pain, paralysis, and even death. "It felt like the flu initially, but by the third day I could hardly get up and was sleeping about twenty hours a day. I couldn't walk, I couldn't feed myself, I couldn't brush my teeth, or even focus my eyes to read. My brain was scrambled, basically."

The family went home for four months and returned to the field before Lisa was really ready; the stress of this was more than she could handle. She also did not realize that a period of depression is normal after a brain trauma.

"I was half crazy; my emotions were up and down. I was pushing myself to do this really hard thing without any support or a team, and I had two little kids! So I wiped out pretty bad. I had a breakdown."

This experience taught Lisa that a willingness to go anywhere and do anything for God was not enough. What did she think she was trying to prove? She now believes that God, in his severe mercy, used the breakdown to bring her whole approach to life into question. "Things you could 'deal with' back home drive you to your knees here," she says. "Being a frontier missionary is a fast track to sanctification."

At the time of her breakdown, the lessons were harder to see. She felt that God had abandoned her. "A couple of years later I started to unpack it and saw that the way I approached life was not healthy. It had to change. I think the reason God let me go through that—let me fall completely apart—was that he needed to show me I needed to learn not to do things by my own strength. At that time of my life I didn't understand grace. I thought I had to do stuff to earn God's approval."

Lisa and Jason made a few changes in their lifestyle; they had to change some things if they were going to stay on the field. They got a car so Lisa could get out of the neighborhood to "go some place else and act different." Nearly once a week she and the kids spent the day at a beautiful international hotel where Lisa could get away, eat whatever she wanted to, and relax while her kids swam in the pool. The family relaxed their standard of living so it wasn't so hard, and made plans to get out of town every few months. None of these changes were ones Lisa could have accepted in the days when she was trying to live the hardest life she could handle.

Life under Pressure

Still, the basic lesson of living by grace instead of performing for God was one on which she'd be tested again and again.

Learning to Rest in God's Presence

Working in a different country and still busy with her children—four of them now, the oldest a teenager—Lisa still struggles to live a healthy, balanced life. "It takes some time. A year and half ago I went home on furlough really tired and stressed out. I was really pushing on language. I wanted to be the best, the first woman on my team to minister in the local language! I was studying with a tutor five days a week; I couldn't keep up the pace. My pastor back home said it was an idol. I think he was right. I wanted to glorify my ego and make sure other people didn't pass me up.

"I feel freer from comparison now. The whole process that God was teaching me before—to rest in his presence—has continued. My one teammate is extremely ambitious, but she's really been sanctified in that. It's her passion to disciple. She was made to teach women. She homeschools well and is a good homemaker, but making disciples is her passion. Me, I love canning and gardening and cooking and reading books to my kids."

Lisa tries to let go of her desire to be the best at everything, and to a large degree, seems to be succeeding. She gives priority to supporting her husband and keeping things running smoothly in the household. And, she says, "If I ever have to choose between ministry and the kids doing well, I would choose the kids every time! This probably sounds bad, but I don't care if I never disciple anybody."

Staying on the Field

Lisa still says she'll go anywhere and do anything for God, but now this is a matter of obedience, not personal pride. She and Jason serve in leadership in their organization and they have also faced criticisms, deserved and undeserved, from teammates also going through struggles. This has tempered them as well. "Jason says, 'The good thing about it being hard is that you keep going only because the Lord asks you to, not because you are getting a lot of affirmation. Hassles keep you before the Lord, which is where you are supposed to be anyway.' Sometimes the only thing that keeps me going is just pure obedience. God told us to be here and that's why I am here. That's all there is to it, because it just isn't any fun sometimes.

"But on the good side of things, we have a really good marriage! And it wouldn't be as good if we hadn't had to go through this. It has sanctified us and made our marriage better. The kids are doing great. They are emotionally healthy and walking with the Lord. If you obey God, even when things aren't fun, you have good fruit in your life. It's really the main thing.

"I can get together and complain with people, but when push comes to shove I have grace to live this life. My journey with God is where it all starts. Before, I wasn't healthy. He fixed me and started teaching me how to live."

28 What God Has Not Promised

Donna, now a missionary in Central Asia and a mother of three, grew up in the church. Her father, whom she considers her spiritual leader, was a pastor. Donna* has had a strong faith for many years. Even so, she sees now that she had many misconceptions about God. The Lord has used the hard things she has been through to help her understand him better.

"One of the things I've been learning in the last few years is to see the things God has promised me, not the ones I wanted him to promise me or thought he'd promised me. And now," she adds, "I would rather have his promises.

"He didn't promise me there wouldn't be pain, for example. When someone is sick or in trouble we pray, 'Please don't let him hurt,' as if God said he didn't want people to experience hurt. Well, he hasn't promised that."

Like Donna, many of the young believers in her host country are eager to believe that God has promised to make their lives easier than they were before. Donna sees them frustrated when the gospel doesn't bring the rewards they expected—for example, an easy life like they believe she has.

"People say, 'Why is God better to you than to us?' I wonder why has God blessed me like this. I've struggled with guilt so much." Although Donna tries to live simply, her husband Kevin is in a high position in the company where he works and is expected to live up to his status. Wealthier Muslim neighbors and Kevin's coworkers approve of Kevin and Donna's lifestyle, but she cannot please both them and the local believers, who tend to be poor and want the gospel to make them rich.

---

* For more about Donna, see chapter 35. What Will People Think?, 44. A Separate Ministry from Her Husband, and 48. Can My Kids Learn This Language?

"Should I have left all my stuff in America? I can't give it all to them, can I? What am I going to do? You pray through it with people, and you teach them the Word, but you can't take away the struggle. What we promise our friends here can't be, 'Follow Jesus, and your husband will convert, you will have a job, and your life and kids will be great.' If you promise those things, it's going to be really hard for them later on." As she teaches local believers about what God promises and what he doesn't, she thinks about how she learned the same lesson herself.

Losing a Father

Donna was in her home country giving birth to twins when her beloved father got sick. "He creaked when I hugged him; I could feel his bones. But I didn't know how sick he was." Eventually his doctors said it was leukemia, but they said he could have five to six years more of life. Only after Donna and her family returned to the field did the doctors realize how serious her father's condition was. "He was dying."

Returning to Central Asia, Donna was overwhelmed by drop-in guests and had no place to go with her fear and grief over what was happening at home. "I had just come back with eight-week old twins and had to put all my energy into hosting. I thought I would probably never see my dad again." Until the week her father died, people were trying to encourage Donna to believe that his condition was curable, that the doctors would find the right medication and he would get better. "I never felt God was going to heal him, though. I had faith about what the Lord can do, but I was trying to be realistic about what could happen." In spite of her commitment to face the facts, Donna realized she was very upset—upset at God.

Kevin and Donna attended a conference on the book of Daniel during this time, and the speaker exhorted them to take the same posture Daniel did, saying, "Our God is able to deliver but even if he doesn't, I'll still worship him."

"I felt it was important that I be honest with God and with people. And to be honest, I was furious!" says Donna. "I just exploded. 'It's not that I think God can't heal my father; I think he can and isn't going to.' I needed God to give me some answers!"

Even though the Lord did give her some answers, the violence of her emotions made her wonder if there was something wrong. "Why does it make me so mad when he won't do what I want him to do?" Could it be that her view of God was false? Realizing this might be the case was the turning point—at least in Donna's view of God. As for her father's health, it continued to deteriorate rapidly.

Donna returned to the States to be with her father and family for a few weeks and was able to spend time with him each day. "He stayed up until eleven the last night I was there, talking to us," she says fondly. "He was so ready to go to the Lord. But it was almost like he felt guilty leaving my mom and knowing what she was going to go through. 'I have been sharing about this Lord and this place, heaven, for forty-two years,' he said. 'What a waste my life would be if I was not now ready.'

They lost him one month later, on Donna's birthday—after she'd returned to Central Asia. Just before he died, she was able to talk to him on the phone. "'I will get on the next plane and come home, but Kevin and the kids will have to say here,' I said, feeling bad about it. I didn't want the family to feel disrespected, but getting five of us on a plane wouldn't happen! But Dad, he had me put Kevin on the phone. 'Thank you for taking care of my grandchildren,' he said." Donna flew out alone this time. "But I didn't make it. Dad died before I got there."

Facing the Loss

"I didn't want to be one of these people who after a death are all smiley and chipper and saying God is good and it's okay. I remember thinking on the way home how disrespectful it would be for me to do that. I want these people to know I loved my dad and that his death had caused a huge gash to be taken out of me!

"But I didn't know how to do this grief thing. I was really hurting. No one here had ever met my dad except for my husband, who only knew him a little bit, and nobody was at the funeral with me. So it was only a loss for me. My twins had just turned one year old, and when I came back to Central Asia after the funeral, it seemed like the whole world was invited to my house as guests." They were only showing their concern and respect, according to Central Asian custom, but it was hard for Donna to take. "'Don't be upset,' they all told me. 'Don't tell me not to be upset!' I wanted to shout, 'I am upset!' It was a really, really hard thing. It helped that I knew the Lord and knew my father was with him. But it still hurt like all get out!"

Feeling unable to express her grief made things worse for Donna. "I couldn't cry in front of the kids, because it would upset them. With three kids, relatives, and guests staying with us, what could I do? I couldn't have quiet times, because I knew I would cry! I had 'ritual' times with God, but I knew if I really engaged with God I would cry. You just get distant from God if you live that way.

"I thought I was obsessed or going insane. I loved my dad so much, but I didn't know why it hurt so bad for so long. It was all very confusing for our marriage. I talked to my husband about how I felt, but he didn't know what was normal either. I would ask him, 'Am I insane?' 'I don't know,' he said. I thought I was a basket case."

Who Has Been through This?

Donna did not know anyone who had been through this kind of grieving process. A few friends in the expatriate community had lost their fathers, but they were children of divorce and didn't feel it the same way. Donna had not only lost her father, but also her pastor, mentor, and spiritual leader. Her loss felt tremendous, and she didn't have anyone to talk to about it.

"Then someone came to the field who had been through the same thing. She said that in grieving she would have two- or three-hour quiet times, and it took forever. It had been a year since his death by this point. 'It will take you three years,' she predicted, and she was right.

"Talking to someone else who had been through it really helped. She let me know it was normal. I had never understood denial, and I wasn't denying that he was gone, but I didn't want it to be true. I didn't want to accept it. I had to accept that it didn't matter what I wanted; the Lord had done it. And I needed to accept what the Lord had done."

What Has God Promised?

"God has promised to walk through this stuff with us," says Donna. "Well, I didn't want to walk through this or be walked through it; I wanted to go a different direction! God promises he will be with us in this world. He didn't promise things wouldn't hurt.

"There is a woman across the street who has a ninety-one-year-old dad. I thought, 'Why does this grumpy man get to live to be ninety-one when my dad only lived to sixty-four?' It wasn't fair! Then the Lord said to me, 'Would you want to have that guy as your dad for ninety-one years, or have yours for sixty-four?' That really helped. You can tell God what you want, but when he tells you there's something better, it's true. You have to see it from his perspective.

"After I had worked that through with the Lord, I knew the Lord was right, and good. I knew I'd bank my life on it. When all the people left Jesus, the disciples still said, 'Where else would we go?' I knew no matter whatever else happened in the world, I had no other place to go but God.

"I couldn't sing those songs like, 'Lord you are good.' It took about a year before I could feel anything in my heart but pain. It was hard. He had kept his promises to me, and they were good. They just were not the promises I thought he had made. I still cry when I think or hear about heaven because I miss my dad so much."

Finally Moving On

Donna finally started to recover. "Then I had to deal with guilt that my dad would have been shamed if he had seen how I had reacted! That was just Satan. You can't ever go back and do it again. I couldn't go back and make my response to my dad's death right, or respond in a more godly way than I did. It's just another thing that can't be undone. It helped to realize that my dad would understand, and that God had forgiven whatever was there.

"My attitude toward God is very different now, and it's easier to accept pain. Now if I lost my mom, I know my response would be different."

The next major crisis that came in Donna's life was not the loss of her mother but a fire that threatened to burn down her house and endanger her children and neighbors. While this was a frightening experience, it revealed that the changes in Donna's perspective had really taken hold.

"I responded differently than I ever would have if it had happened before my father's death. It was just the Lord. I was terrified, but I said, 'Lord, whatever you are going to do, it's okay.' I prayed that my kids would get out okay and that none of the neighbors would be hurt, but I did not beg. I could ask; I could accept."

Donna was grateful she did not have to bear the loss of anyone close to her that time, but the time will come. Grief is never easy, but now she has come to terms with the fact that while God is good, he has not promised to spare her pain and loss. It makes a difference in her ministry, as she shares about the Lord with local believers and others. God has made this a growing experience for Donna.

Her father would be proud of her. "That's what my dad would want, for me to grow."

29 Taking a Backseat to Local Believers

Seven years ago when Ann* came to Southeast Asia as a church planter, she had a full team to work with, all members of her home church. God had answered so many prayers as everything came together. The team prayed and prepared, studied language and Islam, and came with strong support from their church. "It looked like it was going to be a great team," she said. "All of us thought we would go into the area, live there, and do direct evangelism."

Over the next few years, however, political tensions in their area grew, until all foreigners were pushed out. Ann had been on the field for five years at that point and found this to be a huge disappointment. Moreover, her great team had fallen apart.

Ann explains, "There were a thousand issues, including a great deal of spiritual warfare I think. Kids' education was part of it, and a lack of mentoring, and differences among us. We really did not know how different our expectations were until we clashed." Over a period of four years, all the team members were taken away until Ann was the only one left, living in a nearby but safe city with a large Christian population.

"I wasn't ready to give up and go home, or to join another team. For a while I was the only one, and that's a situation I wouldn't recommend to anyone. But for two years I kept the doors open until my new team came together and showed up."

Dealing with Unmet Expectations

"I was angry at God, actually. Unity is supposed to be what we are about, so how could this have happened? I did not understand. There was a lot of loneliness in that. There were huge wilderness

---

* For more about Ann, see chapter 17. Choosing Your Friendships and 40. Life and Leadership as a Single Woman.

periods when I didn't feel met by God or understand what he was doing.

"I made a decision to go to the field based on things that ended up not coming true and had a huge period of grief," says Ann. She went from an immersion situation, living and working among the people she hoped to reach, to dealing with a Christian culture she did not much like. As a result, she says, "I've dealt with more culture shock in the last two and half years than the first five.

"We come overseas with such a romantic idea of what it's going to be like. Everyone I have known who went through what we did has had to go through a very significant mourning period. Your expectations are torn out from under you. I was kicking and screaming for at least a year about the move. I was very resentful, and the others felt the same.

"Then I got to a point of letting go, saying, 'Okay, I guess we have to do this.' Even, 'Yes, maybe there really is something here for us.'"

Team, Task, and Trust

Now a new team is forming, and Ann has happily handed over the reins to a new team leader. Yet the new team has challenges of its own. "We have not had a major argument, but we have different perspectives and have to work though these things. After seven years I have ideas about where we're going and how to get there; I see certain methods as being more effective than others. Everyone does. You have a passion for certain things and want to push in those areas. And we do not always agree."

Some of the tensions have to do with their "exit strategy," how the team will know when their work is done. Ann thinks they should stay until the church in their focus culture is planted and reproducing. A teammate says the job will be done when the partnership between the foreigners and the believers they are training is well established. "It could be a ten-year difference," says Ann, concerned.

"Well, we're trying. Even with maturity and experience, we come at strategy from different assumptions and perspectives. We must be committed to hearing one another out and seeking God's heart on the issue. I do feel this team is more mature, and we are able to discuss and work through our different perceptions better than the previous team. And I know the team leader is committed to hearing the team members.

"We all had images of what was going to happen. You can't come to the field without expectations or assumptions, and you need to talk about things and work them through."

One thing that has brought Ann's idealism into balance is seeing that she is not working in a closed system. Even if she finds great unity on her team, what she refers to as "God's team" (all the national believers and Christian workers in her city and region) may be quite diverse and approach things differently from one another.

Christians from other teams and countries were reaching out to her focus people and sending in short-term teams. What they do, whether it is well conceived and successful or not, affects everyone's work. That may seem like good news some times and bad news other times. "You aren't going to keep it 'pure,'" says Ann. "You can't think you're going to go in and do it your way because other churches, teams, and individuals are involved with their own perspectives, ideals, and dreams."

Another foreign worker in Ann's city is from a different ethnic background and has struggled as well. "It's his way or no way. He's so opinionated. He had his ten-year church-planting plan and a business plan, and he was going to stay on target no matter what. The people he hired were going to start making money in six months or they would be out. I thought he'd crash and burn and he has, almost. He's quite honest about that. When he went home on furlough, he was depressed as heck. He thought Southeast Asians were stupid and a waste of time."

His agency sent him back to the field with different orders, and while his personality has hasn't mellowed much, he sees things differently now. This man, says Ann, is part of God's team, and he is still learning, too. Even when his attitudes and approaches seem strange to her, Ann has to accept that he is part of God's plan. We do not know how God is going to accomplish the work. "We need to be multiplying ourselves. We need to have more people doing evangelism—all kinds of people."

Mobilizing National Believers

Since they cannot live among the people they want to reach, Ann and her team now work hand-in-hand not only with other foreigners but especially with Southeast Asian believers. They come from a variety of backgrounds, are able to share the gospel with other people groups, and can get into places a westerner cannot. There is great promise in this strategy. It's also messy, though. Young churches everywhere have many of the same problems. Immature leadership, status struggles, and overconfidence plague some Southeast Asian believers and churches.

In some ways the Southeast Asians are at a disadvantage compared to the westerners. Few of them come from Muslim backgrounds and sometimes have more prejudice than patience toward the cultures they are not reaching out to. "We've had the time, the training, and the preparation to recognize how ethnocentric we might be. They haven't. When they see an aspect of the culture they don't like, they may just say, 'I'm not going to do that, the culture will just have to adjust to me!'"

Ann is afraid they will not love the focus people the way they need to be loved. "They treat relationships as a project, you know, saying, 'I'm going to witness to so many people in the next month.' Relationships are pursued because of a need to witness rather than to truly enjoy a person."

The local Christians Ann works with do speak the national language fluently, which is a huge advantage. In some ways, their cultures are closer to that of the people they are trying to reach. On the other hand, this may make going the extra mile to really learn the local language as difficult as humbling themselves to understand the culture. "They hit the level where they just think, 'This is ridiculous. I can't communicate what I want; I'll just use the trade language.' That barrier may need to be crossed," says Ann. On the other hand, she realizes that if the Southeast Asian Christians can succeed as evangelists, enough members of the

Muslim community may become believers that the church will naturally be established in *their* heart language. "We really do not know how this is all going to work," she says.

What is clear is that seeing the church planted is going to take much more creativity, perseverance, and partnership than Ann and her team had perceived at the beginning. "And, I think, a lot of failures! I heard a guy speak at a conference who had been working within a Muslim group for thirty years; he talked about how many works he had started that came to nothing!" When Ann told these stories to the Southeast Asian believers she works with, they said he probably didn't do things "right." They don't realize he could have been doing everything right and still fail. Many Western teams have crashed and burned, and Ann believes some of the teams made up of Southeast Asians will too. They are just starting to experience the kind of team conflicts she went through, conflicts they thought they would never face. At times it must be hard for Ann not to say, "I told you so."

It's only human to want to shape the way the church emerges and to stake a claim on it, but Ann and her team may have to give up that dream. They are still working to see the people group they love reached with the gospel, but they often do not even get to meet the new believers. The political situation is still rather tense, and Ann cannot even visit the area where the focus people group lives. She can only help train others who will reach them. Ann and her team have to take a "backseat" behind the national believers and may never get any credit for their work. All this is very humbling. Yet Ann holds onto this: it is a privilege to be part of "God's team," no matter what one's position.

Discussion Questions for Part 3

Chapter 22: The Cost of Compassion

1. How do you tend to respond to the sick and needy? Are you comfortable with your response? If not, what attitudes and temptations do you need to guard against?

2. How can you respond to people who demand more than you can give? How can you best glorify God in this?

3. What experience do you have praying for people through their troubles, rather than trying to fix them? Who do you know who does this well?

Chapter 23: Available in the Busiest Season

1. Compare Vivian's story with Jennifer's in chapter 22, "The Cost of Compassion." Jennifer set boundaries where Vivian accepted pressures. How do you think you would respond in each of these situations?

2. At what point have you found you need to take the first route and set boundaries? When is it better to accept the demands of others?

3. What helps you know the difference?

Chapter 24: Does God Want Us Overseas?

1. Share ways God has provided for your needs through others you know in times of debt, loss, or confusion. What does he want you to remember about these experiences?

2. What trials have you faced that have seemed to put you off the course God had for your life? Have you seen God redeem some of those detours?

3. Discuss your philosophy of calling or gifting for ministry. Do you agree with Sally's perspective? How has God shown you where he wants you and how he wants to work through you?

Chapter 25: Commitment under Crisis

1. What strikes you most from Ginny's story? Have you ever thought about how you might respond in a situation like hers?

2. What experiences have helped you appreciate your family and the other blessings you have?

3. Share an experience that demonstrates the importance of prayer support.

Chapter 26: Sickness

1. How do you tend to respond when your husband or child is sick? How do you want people to respond to you when you are sick?

2. To what extent are you willing to have someone with chronic illness on your team? To what extent do you think a team should be responsible for someone who is seriously ill?

3. What are some ways you have seen God glorified in your weaknesses?

Chapter 27: A Fast Track to Sanctification

1. What stands out to you most from Lisa's experience? What are some ways you can identify with her?

2. Share some ways you have tried to impress God or others. What principles or examples have tempered this and taught you about God's grace?

3. What are some ways you still need to grow?

Chapter 28: What God Has Not Promised

1. How have you seen your own tacit expectations of God revealed? Do you tend to expect things of him that are not appropriate?

2. Share a story about a grief or loss you have suffered, and what was helpful to you or what lessons you learned.

3. What would you do if one of your parents died or suffered a major illness while you are on the field? Have you discussed this with your team, agency, and family?

Chapter 29: Taking a Backseat to Local Believers

1. Have you ever been forced to make a major change in ministry strategy, as Ann did? How did this affect you emotionally?

2. What have you learned about working with missionaries from other backgrounds who approach things very differently than you do?

3. What struggles might local believers face in reaching nearby people groups that you would not face? What things might be easier for them?

Part 4:
How Should We Live?

Questions of Culture, Values, and Money

30 Suddenly Rich

"Our neighbors are super poor," explains Jennifer.* Gifted in compassion, she and her husband Robert feel called to live among the neediest people in their city. In the Central Asian country where they have spent their last seven years, it is possible to live at the level of the people—some of the people. But in this part of town, neighbors may always see Jennifer and her family as the rich foreigners. "We want to relate to them. Even though we sort of hide what we have, we really do have the money to get whatever we want. At home we were the poorest people we knew, and here we're the richest!"

Laurie, one of Jennifer's neighbors, has a husband who drinks. The family never has much money. But she and Jennifer have become good friends, and Laurie is now a strong believer in Christ. The two women see a lot of each other. They talk on the phone frequently, and Laurie will visit Jennifer at home, often coming to pray with her in the evenings. Jennifer rejoices at all she has in common with Laurie, but now and then something will come up that emphasizes the differences between them. That's when Jennifer squirms.

Something that seems small to Jennifer may be unattainable to her local friends. "We had two fans for the kids' room, not very good ones, and they both broke. Cheap ones break so easily. The room was so hot, though, that we decided to buy them a 'good' fan. We paid $60 for it. Otherwise the kids would be lying in a pool of sweat! Laurie's family knew about the broken fans and asked if the kids were okay with such hot weather. Robert told

---

* For more about Jennifer, see chapter 16. An Abundance of Friendships, 22. The Cost of Compassion, and 50. The Perils of Parenting Preschoolers.

them, 'Oh, they're doing all right. We went out and bought them a little fan.'

"'Robert, that was a lie; it isn't a small fan, it's a great fan!' I told him," exclaims Jennifer. "He did not mean to lie, but he definitely gave the impression that we were just getting by." Jennifer knows her husband had great motives: he did not want Laurie to feel bad. He was covering up their differences out of love. But Jennifer was uncomfortable. It was, after all, deception.

Some of Jennifer's teammates and friends in ministry live in wealthier neighborhoods and do not feel the contrasts as keenly.

Challenged to Live Simply

Jennifer would like to see her family live simply. After all, if they truly lived at the level of the people around them, these tensions would disappear. "If we really lived according to the 'incarnational theory' (living out the gospel in a way that is as close as possible to the way local people live), we would get rid of our fridge and everything," she explains. "We would live as poor, so they might become rich—with the gospel."

On the other hand, Jennifer recognizes that living at the same level as her poor neighbors might take away all the energy she has for ministry—and for homeschooling her two young children. She and her family want to stay long-term and have something out of which to give. "It's so hard! Without house help, for example, we would hardly see the kids, what for cooking and washing all the time. We would have no time and energy to do anything but just live."

After reading a book that challenged missionaries to live at the level of the people they are ministering to, Jennifer heard someone say that because locals expect missionaries, as westerners, to have a lot of money, they will be suspicious of them if they live too simply. The locals may think you are hoarding it greedily or that you are "up to something." In a culture where simple living, though necessary for some, is not a value, trying too hard to live like the locals may erect more barriers than it tears down.

What, instead, Jennifer wondered, would it look like to live as a "righteous rich person" in such a community?

How Should We Live?

Setting Boundaries

If Jennifer and her family live "above" the level of their neighbors, how will that affect their relationships? What do they do with their "stuff"? Should they try to keep it hidden from local eyes? Maybe, but with kids, this can be difficult.

"Some of our teammates were always having people go through their stuff. That's why they decided to set up their house so their own area is completely separate. They didn't want neighborhood moms asking 'Can I have this toy for my child? Yours have so many!'"

Jennifer, too, has some part of her house that she tries to keep private. "We are in the middle of a discussion about boundaries in the house, especially for the kids. A lot of kids here have lice and fleas, and I'm not sure I want them in my kids' room!" she admits. "It's hard, too, when the neighbors come to play with the toys, not the kids! Should we let the kids decide if they want their friends in here, or what toys they share and what they put away? Or do we make a rule?"

When she cannot or does not have the same things or live the same way as her local friends, it probably is best to keep some things hidden, Jennifer realizes. She does not want her local friends to confuse her family's standard of living with what it means to follow Christ. She also knows that the little things that help her "make it" here do not make much sense to some of her local friends. Sometimes it is better not to share what others can't appreciate—unless you are willing to face the consequences.

"For example, when I was pregnant and needed something to help keep my hypoglycemia under control, I spent a whole day making trail mix. I cracked and cleaned so many nuts—the walnuts are not easy!—and picked all the stems off the raisins. Then the local girls who were staying with us came home. They started into it, just pigging out! 'Stop!' I said. 'Slow down, at least! This is special food!' They just laughed at me and made a huge joke about it from there on out. They thought it was hilarious. 'Slowly, slowly, special food!'"

Jennifer has learned that often her local friends don't like the "special foods" sent in care packages or picked up in the city. When there is something they do like, they eat it all at once. Saving for later is not a cultural value. Jennifer has found that if she cannot share with a generous heart, it may be better to keep some things to herself.

31 Life in Seclusion

While people in many parts of the Muslim world are religiously moderate, Ginny* has been living in one of the cities in South Asia where many of the stereotypes about uneducated, impoverished, fundamentalist Muslims tend to prevail. "I remember in 1998 when we first came to scout it out," she says. "My first impression was, 'Golly, where are all the women?' You scarcely see women outside. It's such a male-dominated society; the women are kept in seclusion, uneducated, and under male control. That is what the conservative movement wants to implement in the whole country. That was quite an awakening, especially living in it.

"Our first house was surrounded by a twelve-foot wall. Here I was with a small child, a year old, and trying to live a contextualized life. That meant I never went out to purchase groceries; we decided Jack would do that, because the men usually do it. So I was stuck in the house. For the first few weeks I was quite miserable, wondering, 'What am I doing here?'

"I couldn't go out and practice my language with everyone, the vegetable seller, the butcher, and baker—like you can in some places. I could go out to get materials for clothes, bangles, or something, with another expatriate lady. But none of my close neighbors would go. Many women are not allowed to go out at all.

"Many women live in very small homes, and it really feels like a prison; they just have little yards and huge walls. Sometimes I felt like I lived in a shoebox. Our second house had a much bigger yard and was a bit more elevated, even though it was on the same street. That gave a different feeling to things. It was just a little bit higher, so I could look out over the wall and see the mountains."

---

* For more about Ginny, see chapter 5. Those Who Persevere and 25. Commitment under Crisis.

Relationship Building

At first Ginny seemed to have no friends and wondered what it would take to change this. "Then the plates started coming. Jack met a young fellow in the neighborhood, and he was a good guy; they started to chat. So he sent home some food for us. I knew that was important; it was an indication that a relationship was desired. I started to visit the family with my little boy, and a good friendship started. I sent back their plates full, usually with cookies or something.

"They had to check me out, first: Is she a good woman? One daughter in this first family spoke English, so I had a means of making myself known. Then they came to my house. I didn't take that for granted. It means something for people from a conservative family to show up at a foreigner's house and continue to come. They trusted me, and they were comfortable in my house.

"We had our house set up in a way they felt comfortable, without furniture in the main room: just mattresses and pillows on the floor, and not many photos or pictures. If we had chairs, some of the women would not know how to sit on them. But it was a nice room. We liked it, and they liked it too.

"They also knew we were honoring their values and traditions. It is not allowed for men to see women who are not in their family. So at first Jack would leave the house completely if the women came; later he would just spend time in another part of the house, but they knew he would never come in where we were. If we visited another family, I would be ushered in with the women and he would sit with the men. They live quite a separate life. There's no interaction."

Adapting the Home

In the most visible parts of her house, Ginny and her family lived in the local style, like the people around them. In other respects they preserved Western ways. "I had a Western kitchen, and that probably blew them away. Some rich people have kitchens, but most people squat around a little kerosene stove to cook. We had a bed, a real bed, and Jack had an office in the

How Should We Live?

house. It was a separate room by the gate. He had men coming in and out, so I couldn't play in the yard with the kids when they were around, but I didn't have to hide in the house. The kids and I could live a pretty normal life."

Although she chafes against the conservative culture at times, Ginny is grateful for the benefits life on the field offers over raising her family in a Western culture. With fewer relationships and activities, they spend much more time together as a family, and she sees this as quite healthy.

Unlike workers in many areas with less-rigid cultures, Ginny has relative privacy in her own home. She does not have as many frequent drop-in visitors. In her home, she follows more Western patterns. Yet she is not unaffected by the society's rules. They seep in when you don't realize it. "One challenge is just for the husband not to fall into that macho, stupid man behavior! I remember once we went to a restaurant and Jack ordered for me. I said, 'No way! Let me choose.' We laughed about it, but it starts to affect you."

Discouragement

It's been a hard year for Ginny. Now she and her family are off the field and trying to live a 'normal' life for a while. "I need restoration to have compassion to reach out to Muslims again. I have to say that's been diminished. Lies are being preached in the mosques; they are telling people things, like Osama bin Laden is just a puppet America is using so it can go against these Muslim countries. Simple people believe this stuff. It makes me discouraged. And there were some other incidents in the last few months that made my heart grow weary of it all."

Ginny has also faced some personal struggles that left their mark. "I thought I had it all figured out. . . . As a woman you don't go out by yourself unless you are with another woman and/or have your kids with you. Then they know you are a woman of good repute. If you break those rules, they can think whatever. So, I have gone to the bazaar with my expatriate friends. It's a bit tense, it's not like going to the mall, but it's okay.

"Then, one day I went out our door and just down the street, alone to return a book to a neighbor. This guy rides by on a bike and grabs me on the breast! I screamed at him; I was so angry, devastated. Jack was with a neighbor, and I called to both of them over the wall. They came out and went off to try to find this guy, but of course he was long gone.

"I was afraid to go out in the neighborhood after that. I was afraid the neighbors were thinking badly of me, too—that I was now considered a bad person in the neighborhood. My close neighbors came to my house and comforted me, though—much more than the expatriate ladies could. 'That was a bad man who did this to you. It was not your fault. It can happen to anyone, not just to you because you are a foreigner. There are bad men in every place. It can happen in any society. It can happen to anyone, not just to you.' That comforted me. 'But,' they would add, 'you see why we can't go to the bazaar.'"

The moment she called for help from her husband's friend, Ginny knew she had reinforced the seclusion of the women in his family. Both the men and women in her friends' families would say, "There are bad men out there; we want our women honored and protected, so they can't go out. The men will do all the shopping, and keep the women safe."

"If something like this happens to a local woman, she probably couldn't tell anyone; she would immediately be put in a position of it being her fault. I was angry, but I could talk to Jack about it."

Event after event made it hard for Jack and Ginny to continue living in their host city. "'Man,' I think, 'I have gone through so much and still haven't seen a significant breakthrough—in anything!'" Ginny knows the kingdom of God does not grow automatically when God's people are "doing everything right," but, on the other hand, she still struggles to know, without fruit, if she is doing things right. It is harder to evaluate. Ambiguity is one of the costs that she, like many others in her situation, has to accept.

32   Evaluating Cultural Values

After living for several years in Central Asia, becoming competent in the local language, and learning to appreciate the culture, Linda* is able to get past the surface level with her friends and talk to them about values. Now she can help them understand the way she lives and the meaning behind what she does or thinks. She can also discover the values behind their actions and expectations. This helps her build relational bridges. "It's all part of the process of discovering what it means to be a good woman here," she says.

"I've learned where my own values lie," says Linda. "I also want to develop local values, or at least understand them, and practice both if possible."

Meeting Expectations

Some local values and practices are easy to embrace. "Like changing into your housedress when you come in from the street, to keep your clothes nice. That's just a good idea! I think we should all do that," she says. It is easy to cheerfully go along with practices that are more sensible than those at home, or to pick up local customs for responding to situations not found in one's home culture.

Other practices and values may be harder to adopt. For example, practicing hospitality is something the Bible exhorts us to do. It is both part of Linda's personal value system and an important part of the local culture. But she cannot go along with all of the local culture's hospitality traditions. Linda sees local friends and neighbors go overboard out of personal pride.

* For more about Linda, see chapter 10. What Keeps Her Going.

A desire to impress their guests and protect their reputations may overshadow any wish to serve or honor their guests. Allegiance to some hospitality practices exacerbates poverty and family tensions. Where Linda and her team value simple living, their host culture encourages people to get and flaunt the best things they can possibly afford.

Is Linda willing to adopt the local practices and embrace the values behind them? Yes and no. She looks for common ground and, when there is variance, tries to make her motives clear through gracious communication. With hospitality, for example, she says, "I want to make sure I'm being both generous and responsible."

Similarly, because Linda's husband is the director of a business, he is expected to have a large house. Linda and Aaron's house is very nice, but it is small. As their family grows they will probably move into a larger house, but they may never live as extravagantly as some friends expect them to.

In other areas, Linda is still testing the waters. As a westerner, she prefers to keep cupboards well stocked instead of running to the bazaar every day or two. At times, this seems strange to her new house helper, Rachel. "I don't want to keep everything out of sight," Linda says. "I want to be transparent with Rachel. As I see her reaction and hear her comments about what I buy and the way I behave and keep house, I can know how things are perceived. Then I'll know what to do differently. I'll see what things I should put away."

Encouraging Creativity

Sometimes honoring the local culture means learning to take things they way they are intended, not as they appear. This may just take time to internalize. For example, according to local tradition, guests are constantly urged to eat. Hosts may be very insistent, although guests need not respond by gorging themselves and would be less respected if they did. A foreigner can quickly feel overwhelmed and manipulated. Linda has learned to put aside such defensive reactions and graciously accept what is offered. "When they are saying 'Eat, eat!' I say, 'Thank you,' even if what

I mean is, 'Thank you for your kindness,' not 'Thank you for the food'!

"'You understand,' is the best compliment I can get from a local friend," Linda says with a smile.

Doing things the local way is not necessarily automatic for Linda, however. She finds it encouraging that her house helper and other local friends think her ways of doing things are good ideas. "I never would have thought of that," they will say and try it for themselves. While she doesn't want to upset the whole culture, Linda likes to take these chances to help her local friends to manage their houses and live creatively.

Along with another woman on her team, Linda has started a "craft club" with local women. For about fifty cents a week Linda's friends can come to her organization's development center where they have learned how to make greeting cards, memory albums, and decoupage. Some simple woodworking is next on the list. "The goal of this is not that the women would learn to do these outsider crafts as much as to have their own creativity honored and stimulated," says Linda. It is a good way to affirm women, build their self-esteem, and encourage them to make their homes more pleasant.

Talking about Values

"When we talk about how to do things, I always try to take it to the next level, to help them think in terms of values," says Linda. When she was growing up, Linda's parents could have afforded expensive cars and televisions and a big house. Local friends might expect that she had those things, but she didn't. "Instead, we used the money we had for travel and education because that was more important to my parents. Here, people put their money into dowries and entertaining."

If local friends look at Linda's photos from home, they may see a few of the women wearing sleeveless shirts or dresses. Many in the city where she lives now would consider that shameful. "They know I won't dress like that here because it would be looked down on. So I tell them, every culture has things it looks down on. I behave respectably here, but it's not because I just think the local ways are better. In fact, if they went to my home culture dressing the way they do here, nobody would respect them!"

In a culture where creative thinking and questioning the "right way of doing things" is subtly discouraged and certainly not taught, Linda has the opportunity to open her friends' minds to new ideas. She is helping them learn to evaluate what they believe and how they want to live. It may be a small step, but this, in itself, is a ministry.

33 Choosing Where to Live

When Connie, her husband, and their young children, who are now grown, first moved to South Asia, they had a hard time finding models for how to set up their house. The singles with their organization were living below the level of the lowest social group in a poor society. Connie* and her husband knew that wouldn't work for them. A local Christian family of five that they befriended was living in a three-room apartment, and that still did not seem like enough. "That wasn't right for our family, either," says Connie. "But what should we do?"

They could not live among the people they were most interested in reaching, a group of refugees, but they wanted to live a life that fit in with local believers and the larger society as much as they could. Eventually, they decided to live in an area with other foreigners, near the international church and the children's school. It may seem like compromise of the principles of "identification" to live in a larger house, clustered together with other foreigners, but for Connie and her family, the decision turned out for the best.

"Three months later riots broke out. The refugees were all shipped ten miles out of the city to a moon-crater of a refugee camp, and the whole city was under curfew. Where we were, with so many foreigners around, turned out to be the safest area."

Struggling with Guilt

"God brought us a really nice house, and I really struggled with that. I felt guilty for the longest time. Especially when other

---

* For more about Connie, see chapter 3. Loneliness and Adjustment and 52. The Right School for Your Kids.

foreigners would come to our nice house and say things like, 'We just wanted to see how the other half lives!' That would just make me cringe." In later times she lived in smaller or less expensive houses, while others lived in nicer places. In both situations she had to learn to accept the disparities and her feelings about them.

"I think lots of women struggle with guilt. If you tend to think that our role is to suffer and live a hard life, it will be mentally hard for you to receive nice things, to have house help, and to spend money on creature comforts. I thought we should live simply and felt bad when things were nice. My husband came from a higher class background, and it was easier for him, more what he was used to. I've had to overcome it. It's easier to do with less if I don't feel guilty about what I have."

Contextualization

When they moved to another city, Connie and her family had the opportunity to adapt their lifestyle to the local context to a greater degree, and she developed a philosophy that has carried over into other settings—as long as her house can accommodate it. "I like to have one or two rooms totally local. So our main living area, our living and dining rooms, were more like middle-class nationals; that was reasonable enough. Our bedrooms, though, were exactly like we liked. That was our sanctuary, and I wanted it to feel like home; I even put cross-stitch on the walls.

"My goal is that people feel comfortable in our home," says Connie. "'People' includes my family and the other foreigners, the middle-class Christian community, and the lower-class local community."

Connie's early efforts at hospitality taught her a few lessons. One she had to learn was that keeping everything simple is not necessarily good contextualization. "I really like the little cups they drink from here. We hunted and found these tiny little clay ones—they were great! But then I realized when we went out to visit people in the refugee camp, they would sit us down and go dig through boxes and find us nice china cups and saucers. They served us tea in the best they had to offer. And here we had gone

How Should We Live?

out and tried to find these cheap little clay pottery ones to make them feel at home!"

Temporary Solutions

Decisions about how to live can be quite perplexing, especially to a newcomer. One way to ease the tension of setting up a culturally appropriate household is to delay settling into a permanent situation. If you can spend a few months after you arrive overseas living in another foreigner's home while they are out of the country, or better yet, live with a local family, you will have time to figure out how people live and what things are available locally, rather than trying to pack everything you might need when you leave for the field or having to do a lot of shopping on your arrival.

"Some families might only be able to manage it for a month, but I recommend that people get some kind of temporary place. During that time, get into as many homes as you can, foreign and local, and see how people use their resources. I think people who come here with kids are in such a hurry to get settled. That should not be such a high value," says Connie. You don't have enough perspective on these things when you first arrive in a new place. "Don't lock yourself in too soon."

34 "To Know God and Know Myself"

"I have been overseas single, married, and as a mom," says Sally, echoing the experience of many women in frontier ministry. When she left the Middle East to have her first child, Sally* remembers wondering, "'What will it be like coming back with a baby?' I could deal with all the dirt and bugs and stuff for myself, but now I would be seeing things through different eyes. I had to mentally prepare myself to handle it."

Some of the cultural values that she had previously been able to ignore became issues, especially concerning children. For example, as in many parts of the world, parents in the Middle East don't put their kids to bed early; children stay up until the parents go to bed. And they may be less concerned about feeding their children a nutritious diet, or have different ideas about what is good or bad for them. Sally had seen her Middle Eastern friends put Coca-Cola in their babies' bottles. And she knew she didn't want to do that.

Now that she was becoming a mom, Sally knew somebody else would be affected by the decisions she made. She had to decide whether she should follow her home culture's values or her host culture's, or to find some compromise position. The "Christian values" she had known at home in the West were not necessarily right and biblical either, she realized.

"It was a good opportunity to figure out what was important to me and why," she says.

---

* For more about Sally, see chapter 21. A Ministry in Baby Season and 24. Does God Want Us Overseas?

How Should We Live?

Convictions and Preferences

"You have to take time to figure out what are your convictions, and what are merely preferences. Ask yourself, 'What things, if I change them, will make me feel compromised and unable to function?'" Sally recommends that women take time to analyze their basic values before they go to the field.

Just as few pre-marital counseling programs would leave out the discussion of values, few pre-field orientations do either. Books, articles, and teachings on these subjects abound. You may not be able to anticipate all the questions that will come up, but you can prepare yourself to work through them.

Understanding the local culture's values in terms of time, relationships, communication, food, and family is only part of the equation. The other is understanding how much you are willing to live by those values. For example, Sally is a morning person. Everyone in her family gets up at six every day. That means going to bed early, something that seems strange to Middle Easterners.

"What should I do? I found if I stayed up too many nights in a row, even doing 'ministry'—if I didn't get the sleep I needed and a good time with God in the morning—I could not function very long. My life would fall apart." Sally decided it was okay to go to bed early even though it wasn't 'cultural.' "I had to set boundaries. I had to ask myself, 'What choices do I need to make to preserve myself and my health?'

"Self-awareness is so important. When I first went out, I made it my goal to know God and know myself," says Sally.

Helping Others Get the Help They Need

Another aspect of knowing yourself is knowing your personality type and learning style—and being sensitive to others who may be different. "There was a new woman who came to our field," Sally remembers. "The day I met her, I handed her three books to read. 'These will really help you get off to a good start here,' I explained, so helpfully I thought! Each time she came to me with a question I'd give her another book. She must have had seven of them by the time I'd known her a week!

"I could tell from her questions, though, that she wasn't reading them. When I asked, she simply explained, 'I've never been much of a reader.' Then I got it. We had a difference in style. Reading was my way of getting information, but not hers. I needed to accommodate my teaching style to her learning style!"

Sally had to extend her commitment to knowing herself to her friends and teammates, as well as people in the local culture where she was serving. She learned to accommodate the help she offered to their ways of receiving it. In a way, serving your teammates in their own style is like contextualizing your gospel message.

35   What Will People Think?

In the Central Asian country where Donna* and her family live, good housewives rise before dawn, take up their brooms, and sweep their yards, sidewalks, and even the street in front of their houses. It's a culture where women pride themselves on their hard, physical labor. Faithfulness in sweeping not only demonstrates their diligence and keeps down the dust, it also welcomes and honors any guests who may come.

"I should sweep," admits Donna. "I did not mean to blow this off, but when we came I had a seven-month old baby. Then it was winter and so cold and dark. Then I was pregnant with the twins. When we came back after they were born, I was up all night with them! So there was no getting up and sweeping," she says with a sigh.

"What's really funny is that my husband loves to sweep. Kevin is something of a perfectionist and loves to bring order out of disorder." This is a bit of a problem though. While getting the sweeping done matters, it's supposed to be work for a woman, not a man. One night Kevin went out at eleven to sweep, hoping nobody would see him. "But at the next neighborhood gathering, one of the women brought it up; she said she had seen him! And actually, they thought it was wonderful, even though they were sure their husbands would never sweep," says Donna with a laugh.

"Something that really affects women here," Donna explains, leaning forward, "is that the values and choices we as believers and Christian families have are opposed to local values. I don't think the men are going to experience it as much as we do. They may feel it, but they are more often looked up to than we as foreign

---

* For more about Donna, see chapter 28. What God Has Not Promised, 44. A Separate Ministry from Her Husband, and 48. Can My Kids Learn This Language?

women are. As missionaries, we enculturate on lots of things in order to be accepted, but we may have different priorities behind those decisions. And we make these decisions as a family, but it's the women who live it out.

"Some of the things we as believers ought to do fly in the face of local values. The biggest one is for me is how much time I spend with my children. They don't do that here."

Different Priorities

While westerners keep their children with them and try to provide them with discipline, stimulation, and consistency, many of Donna's neighbors focus on getting their kids into preschool at two or three years of age so they can go back to work. The kids often get more positive attention, structure, and stimulation in the school situation than they would at home, so the women think they are doing something good for their children. Those of us from cultures where people assume that mothers should stay home with their children if possible may have a hard time understanding this perspective or even assume it means the moms do not love their children. Likewise, local mothers may think the foreigners are doing the wrong thing.

Missionary women like Donna also add to their roles as wives and mothers a commitment to spiritual disciplines, language learning, ministry, and team life, as well as trying to stay in touch with family, friends, and supporters back home. These aspects of their lives may be invisible to local friends. "I wonder, do they think I'm lazy?" asks Donna. "They don't see all the things we do, so they may not understand how I can say I 'don't have time' to teach their kids English."

Nobody has ever said anything to Donna about neglecting her sweeping, but she wonders what the older women are thinking. In spite of a commitment to relationship building, respecting the local culture, and contextualization, she has to face the humbling reality that she will never get it all "right" in the eyes of her neighbors. "We are going to end up making choices that make us look bad to locals," she says.

An Emotional Issue

Some workers don't do anything to make their family life more local, while others are "all local," says Donna. Many young moms are haunted by a fear that they are getting the balance wrong. Plus, there's the tendency women have to compare themselves to each other and get defensive about their differences. It all adds up to a very emotional situation.

"Sometimes I'm afraid the kids may not get the attention I'd want to give them. But I'm also afraid of using the kids as a shield or excuse not to contextualize or do ministry."

Donna didn't really think she would "hide behind" her kids, but she wondered if others might think that's what she was doing if she gave too much of her time to them. When she would sit on the floor playing with her toddlers, she'd wonder if she ought to be working on her language learning, doing ministry activities, or even sweeping, like her neighbors!

"That's a pride issue. I was neglecting my kids out of pride! God convicted me. He said, 'You enjoy your kids—and keep your ministry fires burning too. Let me help you keep that balance, and don't let yourself worry about what others think about it.'

"I was tired of the pressure of being a missionary," says Donna. "I just wanted to take a break. I wanted to be a godly mother and wife and Christian in this city and neighborhood. So this year that's pretty much all I'm doing. I love this year. It feels totally different."

In addition to making time for her kids, Donna spends time with her husband. This also is contrary to the local culture, where husbands and wives seldom have much of a friendship. But Donna and her husband have a standing lunch date every Thursday. They started this practice when their twins were small. "I told my husband, 'I have to get out; I have to talk to you without a kid!' The men at his work laugh a bit, but they think it is kind of fun that he has a wife that he'd want to see."

Donna knows there are still walls between her and some of the local people she'd like to befriend. The time she has to pray and study may seem like a luxury to local believers. Some women are jealous of the freedom Donna has to stay home with her kids instead of going back to work. They may not have a choice. And unbelievers may not listen to her if they feel she isn't one of them. "The fact that I have a good marriage can be a barrier. When I share the gospel they say, 'But you have a good husband!' They aren't seeing that he is a good husband because he has the gospel." What she hopes is usually a good witness can also be a barrier

Sympathetic Friends

How can a woman overcome the feelings of defeat that come from knowing she doesn't measure up to the culture's expectations for her? One way is to find a few sympathetic local friends. "My housekeeper sees the most," says Donna. "She really appreciates my values. It was weird for me that while she was doing my housework, here I was, this rich lady, playing with kids! But that was the point of having house help, really, so I could study language and invest in the kids. After we had been here a while, she told me she thinks that's really great. I have tried to develop a few relationships with other people who would take the time to understand, people I don't feel judged by. You find the ones who think what you do is good, and you latch on to them. Then I try to keep my perspective based on what they say."

Another supportive local friend, one of Donna's neighbors, helped her find a way to decorate her house in a way that was simple and comfortable, yet elegant enough to suit her situation in life and look attractive to local friends.

Because they live on a busy street, Donna and her husband wanted to make their yard a pleasant place for their kids to play. Even though the concept of a lawn is foreign to their adopted culture, they knew their kids would enjoy it. So they asked their sympathetic friends about it. "I knew grass in our yard might seem weird. When we explained what we were thinking, though, they respected that we made the choice for our kids' sake. We haven't had any grief about it, and I don't think it affected our reputation in the neighborhood at all."

Women who don't have supportive local friends around them to help them navigate their decision-making—and pick their battles—

are the ones who struggle most with guilt and uncertainty. "My goal is not to be a local, because I'm not. Jesus did not enculturate; he incarnated. It's different. But I ask, 'What are the things that will help them feel I came close?'"

36   The Comparison Trap

"I just love it when Michelle wears her blue jeans," says Angela,* an American missionary and mother of four in Central Asia. She's talking about a fellow worker in her city. "Our agency is more conservative, and so are the people we work with. When I first came I wore the local clothing styles everywhere, and I still do around the house, like my neighbors do." After four years, while she still does not wear blue jeans, Angela has picked up a few subtleties and loosened her standards. "The locals put on Western clothes to 'dress up' when they go places, and now I do the same. When we go outside the city to villages, I put my traditional dresses back on."

Deciding how to dress, what kind of food to serve, what to buy or own, and how to set up a home are questions every family living cross-culturally deals with. These questions are part of identification—living like the people you serve so you can better understand them. They are also part of contextualization—living life in ways that help the people you serve better understand you. Both help Christian workers share their faith and model godliness. In many cases, the day-to-day impact of these decisions falls more on the women than the men. This can be a heavy weight to carry, as Angela has found.

"Your first term, you are likely to come at it from one extreme or another," says Angela. "Either you make little effort to accommodate the local culture for fear it isn't godly or that you won't be able to survive, or you give up everything you know and become a slave to local expectations. Making these initial decisions is only half the battle, she has discovered. The rest is

---

* For more about Angela, see chapter 4. Are We Staying or Going?

How Should We Live?

fighting off the guilt that you're doing it wrong, staying open to change, and holding back from comparing yourself to others.

Should You Live like Your Neighbors?

Sometimes the people you compare yourself to are local friends and neighbors. Angela's Central Asian neighbors may envy her relative wealth, but if she chose to live at the simplest level she could, she fears they would be suspicious of her. What is she trying to hide? "They have no concept of simple living. That's one of *our* ideals. If we didn't have more than they do, they would wonder what was wrong with us; 'Couldn't your husband find a job in the States?' I don't want to use that as an excuse to have everything we'd want, but there's a level of tension: they would have what we have if they could."

Many missionary women in Angela's region go back and forth between one way of life and another, sometimes simply by setting up part of the house in a more Western style and part according to the local ways. Angela's city is not so traditional that the difference is great however. "All my neighbors have couches, so that's not a major issue. In our city it's okay to have a little bit more stuff than in some places."

Angela's house is not big enough to have separate quarters for guests and family, however. For her first few years on the field, embarrassed that her way of life was different from that of her neighbors, she kept a cover over her washing machine. Washing machines are considered something of a luxury, and maybe a sign that a woman is too lazy to do the hard work of washing clothes. Angela decided this did not matter and stopped hiding hers. "It began to seem silly, a matter of false pride and a hindrance more than anything."

Making Comparisons

More than comparing themselves to local friends and neighbors, many women in missions struggle with comparing themselves to other workers, for example those who may not have the same family demands. Married women who came to the field single or without children remember how much they used to get done in those days. Women whose ministry or convictions cause them to choose a more conservative lifestyle (for example, in some places, wearing a headscarf) may feel jealous or judgmental toward those who follow more modern or western ways, while the latter may struggle with guilt or defensiveness.

Often it's about money. Some workers live on less than others, by their choice or the choice of their team or agency. Some buy more prepared or imported food, or fancy electronics, or more toys for their children than others can or feel they should. Some spend more money for vacations or trips home; others seem to be just getting by. Many workers feel wistful and neglected when someone else receives more support, monetary or otherwise, from their sending agency, supporting churches, or family back home. Even the most mature believer may struggle with jealousy or discontent over such inequalities.

Maybe such feelings are inevitable when you find yourself doing the most difficult things you've done in your life, says Angela. You are bound to feel insecure. But in such a situation, putting those feelings in their place is more than extra-credit spirituality—it is essential. "Learning not to compare everything is so important," says Angela. "There are so many ways people compare! Be satisfied with what God has given you and where he's put you; wait on him to make use of what you have." The bottom line: choose not to judge one another.

Allowing room for other people to make different decisions may help. While friends who have been in ministry for a while can give new workers wise advice about how to live on the field, says Angela, leaders, teams, and agencies should be careful what things they mandate. Where to draw the lines is not an easy question. Angela would like to see more people in her agency live simply and wonders if the agency should do more to encourage this. But she also recognizes there may be different answers for different people.

"When we set team rules we have to be careful to allow for individualization. In the same town, even on the same team, something might work for one that won't work for another. One woman may be able to have an expensive house, and because of her love for local friends, it's not a hindrance. It would be with me, I think. But on the other hand, if I lived totally like my

How Should We Live?

neighbors, who are poorer than I am, I would only last a year and that wouldn't be good."

Finding Joy

Struggles over issues of lifestyle and comparison can create great stress and rob a believer's joy, and that's the root of the issue, says Angela. "You can only live under great stress for so long; you have to make decisions to take away that stress." If that means having more than other people, so be it.

Another principle Angela has found freeing is that lifestyle decisions don't have to be forever. "You have to say, 'For now, this is what we are going to do,' because things change. Next year we may need less or more in certain areas. Every year is new. Each year we have to discern, 'This is what we need to have joy this year.'

"If survival is all we are doing, we're not doing what God wants us to do. We know several families in town who are doing what they have come to do, and doing it well, but they have no joy! God doesn't want us to live that way. Our first years here, there was no joy, so we've struggled with that ourselves. You've got to have the joy!"

Angela suggests that one thing women can do to maintain a balanced perspective on lifestyle issues is to build a support network that includes people who are not from the same background, not part of your ministry team, and may not be bound by the same expectations. Michelle, the missionary who lives across town, really helps Angela maintain her perspective. Yes, Michelle who wears the blue jeans. Because Michelle is a friend and not a teammate, Angela feels a freedom with Michelle that she might not with some of her teammates. Michelle is different, and Angela can accept that without judging or comparing herself to Michelle. She is outside of Angela's team culture and can talk things over from a slightly different perspective. Plus, Michelle is fun to be with. "Maybe once a month we get together. We may talk about team stuff, but it's good to have someone you don't work with and can just enjoy!"

37

An Answer to My Prayers

"Jacob was a baby when Deborah came," says Catherine,[*] who works in Central Asia. "I was feeling overwhelmed with three small kids and trying to keep a house, and my health wasn't good. I was praying that God would somehow provide help for me. The next day Deborah showed up at my door.

"'Hi,' she said, 'I was wondering if you would consider taking me in to live with you. I'll do whatever you say, but I want to learn English.' I was trying to learn the local language, so at first I thought I didn't want someone who wanted to learn English. But maybe this was God's way of answering my prayer."

Many people would rule out the idea having a local live with them, thinking it would be too stressful, but Catherine knew she needed the help—the benefits outweighed the costs. Deborah went to school part of the time she lived with Catherine's family, but she also helped with the housework and children, much as a daughter might.

Unlike a long-term foreign visitor, Deborah would not need to adjust to her own culture. In fact, she could help Catherine adjust. Catherine found the relationship gave her a window onto the local culture, a valuable opportunity for a woman busy with a family and just beginning to learn the language. "For a woman with small kids who isn't getting out of the house as much as she wants to, there are big benefits to having someone local live with you. You can't be a part of other people's lives as much as a single person might be able to. Finding ways to get into those networks and relationships helps you understand what your local friends think

---

[*] For more about Catherine, see chapter 26. Sickness, 39. Help with House Help, 47. Helping Your Kids Feel Heard, and 53. One-Room Schoolhouse.

How Should We Live?

about and what their hopes, fears, and concerns are. I learned a ton, and also met a lot of people through Deborah."

In addition to learning from Deborah, Catherine enjoyed the chance to minister to her—also something of a rarity for Catherine's stage of life. "If you incorporate someone into your family, she gets to learn all your little traditions and how you think, which is more than a regular house helper would," she explains. "You have more normal interactions, sharing meals and chores. She could see our values and how we did things. It was all very natural according to the local culture. And we never paid Deborah a cent," says Catherine.

A Preview of Raising Teenagers

Although Deborah was indeed an answer to Catherine's prayers, the relationship did bring a few unexpected conflicts. One, as might be expected from someone trying to learn English, was pressure to help her get a visa to work in Dan and Catherine's home country in the West. They did try to help her, but like many of their other friends who wanted to work overseas, she applied and lost her money when her visa was denied.

"We treated her like any teenaged daughter; that's what we called her. We gave her advice and restrictions. At one point she wanted to wear shorts, but because other girls in the neighborhood don't, we said no; there was a big thing about that. By the end of her time, she did a total turnaround in that respect and was dressing much more Muslim."

A more serious problem arose concerning Deborah's choice of friends. When a young man, Deborah's second cousin, started coming around, she would talk with him by the front gate. "We had to restrict that, because it looked bad to our neighbors," says Catherine.

As time went on, the relationship went far beyond talking at the gate. Deborah became emotionally and sexually involved with the young man. The two often fought bitterly, however, and Catherine tried to help Deborah see how controlling he was. But Deborah really wanted to marry him. They were secretly wed, in a religious ceremony though not a civil one. Neither set of parents knew about the marriage, but a sympathetic sister let them meet at her house.

"She did officially marry him and everything, eventually. The whole boyfriend thing was a bigger problem than the pressure about going to America! He was a relative, a second cousin. We had met him when we took her on, but because he was her cousin, we didn't expect this. We actually learned a lot. It was a preview of raising teenagers!"

Learning from Experience

In spite of the difficulties she faced, Catherine recommends that workers maintain an open posture toward inviting locals to live with them. Following a few guidelines can help make the relationships profitable.

The fact that Deborah's motivation for living with Catherine's family was to learn English could have been a burden, but Catherine worked to prevent this. "We laid down restrictions: we spoke the local language during the days, no English. That way the kids and I could benefit from speaking the local language. We would do devotions with the kids in English in the evenings, and Deborah was there for that too.

"I didn't want to be bogged down with having to teach her English, but the more I could teach her, the more I would learn the local language. For example, when I explained in English how to cook for my family, she would repeat what we were doing back to me in the local language. As long as we could do that, even when we were speaking English, I was still learning."

Before Deborah moved in, Dan and Catherine talked to her parents. Deborah had good relationships with her family. Deborah's grandmother, who lived nearby, allowed Deborah to stay with her when Dan and Catherine's team had meetings or other guests. She didn't have to rely on Catherine to be her support system. "It wasn't like we'd be putting her out on the street; she had someplace else to go, so there was freedom for both of us," Catherine explains. "It's also nice to have someone who can go home every weekend.

"There wasn't an expectation that it would be forever, either.

We initially said we'd try it for two weeks, but it went on for a year or so. If it stops benefiting one of you, and you need a change, you want to have that flexibility. You don't want to take someone on permanently or right away. But you can see a lot about how it's going to work out in the first two weeks."

38 Hiring a House Helper

Laura is a young missionary from Australia and still making the transition to motherhood. She and her husband Daniel are part of a church-planting team in Central Asia and delighted with their first daughter. Grace is still a baby, but her birth has forced Laura* to rethink how she wants to use her energy each day. "Shortly before I went home to Australia for Grace's birth," says Laura, "a local friend asked me, 'Are you going to get someone to help you around the house when you come back?' I was a little surprised by her question and wanted to know why she was asking. But she said she thought I'd need the help."

At first Laura thought it might make her look lazy if she hired someone else to do her housework, or part of it. It's something she would never do back in Australia and was not very common among her local Muslim friends, either. "As I thought about it, though, I realized that there are often at least two women (mother-in-law and daughter or daughter-in-law) to do the housework in most local households. Even in the middle-class apartment block where we live, at least half the households consist of more than a nuclear family. Most of my friends call on younger sisters or nieces or girls in their neighborhood for help."

Realizing that most of her neighbors had a source of house help and that some of them would also hire an outsider, at least occasionally, gave Laura the freedom to hire someone to help her, too.

---

* For more about Laura, see chapter 6. Marrying In and 43. Allowing Your Marriage to Change.

How Should We Live?

Discovering What She Wanted

Even before Grace was born, one of Laura's teammates went on furlough and left her house helper in need of money. Laura had a chance to try things out by hiring Mary one day a week. "I got an idea of what it was like to have someone working in my home, how much work I could actually provide, and what kind of person I was looking for. Since I was pregnant, Mary did a lot of the heavy work for me, like sweeping and washing floors, and also some of the things I didn't like to do, like washing dishes after we had hosted a lot of guests. Mary loves doing dishes!

"But even with language study and a lot of visitors, I really didn't need a house helper right then; it was more a luxury at that stage and a help to Mary. But it was fun! I'd mastered cooking the basic local dishes by that stage, but I got Mary to teach me to make the more special ones; we both really enjoyed it."

One great thing about the arrangement Laura had with Mary was that it helped her get used to having an employee. Like many women, she had never experienced that and felt uneasy about hiring a "servant."

"It felt really funny at first. Coming from a very egalitarian society, I felt a bit like a 'white oppressor' having someone doing menial work for me. And I kind of felt guilty asking her to do all the jobs I hated. Well, not all—I still don't ask my house helper to clean the bathroom and especially not the toilet." She also makes sure to treat the girl who helps her with friendliness and respect. "I just can't bring myself to say, 'Oh, you're here, good, get to work.'"

Laura decided that in her host culture, where age and authority generally go together, she would prefer to hire someone younger than herself. So when she came back from furlough she hired Bonnie, a young Central Asian believer and the daughter of some local friends. "It also makes it easier to explain to my neighbors. Bonnie works well for me. She's young enough for me to feel like I can manage her easily. She does her work thoroughly and shows quite a lot of initiative. She loves Grace and is very good with her; I'm quite comfortable to leave Grace with her for an hour or so. Bonnie is here twice a week; Grace thinks she's part of the family."

"I usually try to do housework alongside Bonnie while she's here—tidying up my own room, cleaning the bathroom, hanging out laundry, or whatever. If Grace is asleep, I usually do language study or computer work or something. I don't want to appear lazy to Bonnie or my neighbors, which is also why I still sometimes sweep outside."

Laura recommends looking at your friends' families for potential house helpers. "I invited Bonnie and her parents over for dinner to talk about it before hiring her, and this created some natural accountability structure as well."

However, Laura did not want to repeat the experiences of friends whose relationships with believing house helpers had turned into discipleship more than housework. "With Bonnie, I try to welcome her warmly, say a prayer for her, and chat briefly—just the standard greeting questions, really. Then she gets to work. We have lunch together and that's our time for chatting. My prayer at the end of our meal usually includes presenting all the things that are going on in her life to God."

Knowing Your Needs

Making the most of having a house helper requires some self-knowledge, says Laura. "Think about what you know about yourself, your husband, your family, and your schedule in this whole process. I like preparing for guests, but facing a mountain of dirty dishes after the preparation and hosting is awfully depressing. So I've decided to have Bonnie come the two mornings after I regularly have guests. This helps me enjoy the hospitality part of our ministry rather than it becoming drudgery. Daniel and I also reserve Friday nights for each other. If I spend all day Friday cleaning, I'm usually too tired to enjoy his company. So I have Bonnie come Friday mornings and take care of the housework. That way I can use my time to cook a special meal or plan a picnic or whatever. Daniel comes home to a neat and clean house and a happy wife—usually!"

Presently, two mornings a week is all Laura wants to have

Bonnie working in her home, but sometimes she hires extra help for specific tasks. Two college-aged girls washed all her carpets recently, and another friend did quite a bit of canning for her. Mary makes her peanut butter and grinds rice. All of these things relieve Laura's stress level.

Laura adds that it is important to have realistic expectations about your house helper. "Realize you'll probably never find the perfect house helper. Bonnie can be too thorough: I don't think she needs to rearrange my cupboard every time she puts the dishes away! But given that I appreciate her initiative in other ways, I don't want to squash it in this area, as long as she's not taking too much time on it."

Laura has heard enough stories about house helpers who take advantage of or betray their employers that she is careful to set up clear expectations and consequences with Bonnie. "I think most of our local friends go through a period of testing the boundaries in their relationships with foreigners. They don't have bad intentions; they just genuinely don't know what to expect from us. But you can start feeling like, 'If I give an inch, they'll take a mile.'" One thing Laura finds that helps is to show local friends that she can be hurt, frustrated, or offended, just like anyone else. She expects to be respected and treated like a real person, even if she is a foreigner.

At the same time, Laura knows she needs to show Bonnie grace. "Bonnie doesn't have a phone. If she turns up half an hour late but with a genuine apology, I say, 'That's okay,' because she is usually quite punctual and always rings from a neighbor's place the day before if she can't make it. If she were habitually late or did sloppy work, I'd have to deal with it."

Managing a Household

Laura is still sorting out her own feelings about employing others to serve her. She still wonders how a "good housekeeper" can hire a housekeeper. "Maybe we need to look for new models of how to go about it than the ones we've grown up with. People's lives are a lot different here than in the West and a lot closer to those of women in biblical times. I've found it interesting thinking over

Proverbs 31 lately and realizing that the role of a housewife back then was a managerial one rather than a menial one. In 1 Timothy 5:14, Paul also urges wives to manage their households. There's a lot of seasonal work in being a housekeeper here: spring cleaning, summer canning, and so on—and it involves a lot of planning and coordinating.

"Personally," she adds with a twinkle in her eye, "I often feel like I'm living in one of L. M. Montgomery's or Laura Ingalls Wilder's books. It helps me to think about what filled Marilla Cuthbert's or Ma Ingalls' days!"

39 Help with House Help

In the six years that Catherine[*] and her family have been in their house, at least six different women have worked for them as house helpers. Catherine, her husband Dan, and their three children have enjoyed and learned from these relationships, and Catherine is eager to pass on the tips that have made her experiences successful. It is a bit unusual to have such turnover, but most of Catherine's house helpers have been young women in their early twenties, women who needed something to do between finishing their education and starting families of their own.

Few local Muslims, unless they are quite wealthy, have house helpers, so Catherine can understand why some missionaries are uncomfortable with the idea. However, like Laura, she found that it was not unusual for local people to hire help now and then. "The first local family we lived with had a house helper. One of our teammates had been hiring help occasionally; when we bought our house, it didn't take long to decide that it was a good idea for us to hire house help too."

Benefits and Drawbacks of Hiring Help

"You could spend every minute of the day doing housework if you wanted to," says Catherine, "and I didn't want to! When the kids were little, I could leave them with my house helper; I could get out for language practice or to visit people. Especially for homeschooling moms, you need to realize that the work you are doing is important. Value yourself enough to give it the attention it deserves. Besides, you can minister to someone else

---

[*] For more about Catherine, see chapter 26. Sickness, 37. An Answer to My Prayers, 47. Helping Your Kids Feel Heard, and 53. One-Room Schoolhouse.

by providing work and friendship to another woman who is trying to make ends meet."

But there are other benefits as well. Catherine's house helpers have been able to assist her with her language learning and provide culture cues like what to bring with you when you visit a friend or what to wear to a certain kind of gathering. "They have also helped me learn how to cook properly! I still cook for my family things they learned to like in the West, but I have to be able to cook local dishes as well. And there is no better way than in my own kitchen, day after day."

In addition, relationships with her house helpers have allowed Catherine an easy avenue for making friends and understanding local values and aspects of local life.

"You come to learn about everyone in your helper's family. It's quite natural to pick up on who's who, their comings and goings, their illnesses and arguments. You get a feeling for the rhythms of everyday life in your host culture. But we often get into deeper things as well. If your house helper voices a real frustration, hope, or desire, you can pray for them in that, or talk through it with them, or bring them a story from the Bible. I learned a lot of the traditions, and superstitions as well.

"And I've continued all my relationships with my house helpers past the time they worked for me. They all seem to think fondly of their times working here, and when they drop in, they say it's just like the old days. Some of them want to work for me again when I am not getting the help I need. So, for example, I have one come and wash my windows and put up the plastic each winter."

Just as she sees into her helpers' lives, they see into hers. "Every one of the house helpers we've had has commented on the way Dan treats me and how I deal with the kids. They see what I do every day, taking care of other people, praying, whatever. They know that I'm a religious kind of person."

Catherine recognizes reasons other foreigners might be reluctant to hire house help. It might seem pretentious or lazy or like it gets in the way of identifying with the lives of local friends. Fears about setting boundaries, security, and simply getting used

How Should We Live?

to having someone else in your home much of the time makes some women hesitant to hire help.

"These are all real and serious concerns. That's why the first year, I would say don't have a house helper. In fact, don't have a house! Live with a local family. In our city, where houses are built for multiple families sharing a courtyard, this is relatively easy—and worth it for the learning opportunities it brings in language, culture, and learning how to do things the way they do. With that under my belt, I was in a better position to make wise decisions when I set up my own house."

Tips for Managing House Help

Catherine had never had an employee before, so some of what she had to learn was quite basic. Teammates advised her to make her expectations very clear. "They tell their house helpers up front that they expect promptness, honesty, and diligence. They tell them up front that stealing will mean they lose their job."

Having a schedule of what you want your helper to do each day can really help. "At the beginning, I was terrible at it," says Catherine. "Even now, sometimes I think of something right after they leave! It's good to have some things that are the same from week to week or that can be done if they run out of other work."

In addition, she recognizes that some house helpers will never be good at the tasks you want done, and it may be best to find someone else to help you with specific projects. "Olivia was the queen of organization; I could give her a shelf or box, and she could arrange it for me. And she was great at dusting, so I made sure that was always one of the things I had her do. Jane can't see very well, so she can't dust. But she loves to sweep. If there are others you can call on, or things you can choose to do yourself, make these decisions with their strengths and weaknesses in mind."

Catherine looks for ways to affirm her house helpers' good work. "I pay them full price for what I consider a day's work. If they finish early, they can leave early, but if things are not done I don't pay them full wage." If you see your house helper's work or level of motivation decline, Catherine recommends you ask the following questions:

1. Am I paying a fair rate? "We pay our house helpers the price of one kilogram of meat for a day's work, so our wages fluctuate with inflation. This works pretty well. Since my husband Dan does the shopping, a month went by when I didn't realize the price of meat had gone up! Lynnette was getting slack in her work; I increased her salary, and she was back up to par. The salaries we pay are more generous than locals would for the same work. You could start with the common rate for unskilled workers, such as people who clean offices. If you also want them to cook, watch kids, and help you with language, you need to be more generous. We usually pay monthly. I keep track on my calendar, when she wants money I'll pay up to that point. Lynnette doesn't ask for advances, although we've told her we wouldn't give more than one week's worth if she did."

2. Am I giving her enough work? "If she is sitting around not knowing what to do while you are out visiting, her motivation will go down. That's where a list comes in; it helps her manage her time. If she is counting on you to tell her what to do, it is more difficult for both of you. For example, if you wait until the last minute to tell her what you want her to cook for dinner, she will have to sit around waiting for it to cook; if she knew earlier, she could have started preparing while she was doing other things and be done sooner. Since we let our helpers go when what we consider a day's work is done, instead of leaving at the same time every day, this works well."

3. Is she sick or stressed out by other situations in her life? Ask questions when your house helper is sick or preoccupied. If there is something you can do to help, you need to know. "Does she just need some aspirin? Is she feeling bad? You should ask! If you need to let her go, look at your list, prioritize it, and let her go home early and rest. Sometimes she may just need to talk, or to make a call to take care of something she's fretting about."

4. Do I need to reiterate my expectations? Catherine's current house helper, Lynnette, has begun to get a lot of phone calls while she's working, so Catherine plans on addressing this, and reminding Lynnette of her expectations. "I should have made this clear, but it hasn't been a problem until now. What I'll tell her is, 'You don't need to ask me, it's fine to get or make calls. But try not to spend more than five minutes on the phone. That's work time.'

"Finally, I want to make sure that having a house helper does not keep me, or my kids, from being industrious. The kids have chores, especially on the weekends, when Lynnette does not come. They need to learn how to be responsible and do things around the house, too."

Discussion Questions for Part 4

Chapter 30: Suddenly Rich

1. Try to put into words your convictions or preferences in setting a standard of living.

2. How do you respond to the judgment, jealousy, or admiration of local friends if you have more resources than they do?

3. What material things do you consider necessary or unnecessary at this time in your life, for your family?

Chapter 31: Life in Seclusion

1. Talk about the restrictions women in your host culture face. What is their attitude toward these restrictions? What is your attitude?

2. How do neighbors build relationships in your host culture? What do you know about the social rules and expectations?

Chapter 32: Evaluating Cultural Values

1. To what extent are you aware of your own assumptions and values? Where are these in conflict with your host culture?

2. What values of your host culture do you most appreciate?

3. Share some creative ways you have learned to adapt, being true to your own values while behaving respectably in your host culture.

Chapter 33: Choosing Where to Live

1. What factors have influenced you in choosing a neighborhood, house, or standard of living?

2. How are your decisions the same as and different from those of other cross-cultural workers you know?

3. What does "good contextualization" look like in your situation?

Chapter 34: "To Know God and Know Myself"

1. Which local practices might conflict with your convictions, and which ones only conflict with your preferences?

2. How can you show respect for local values even if they aren't the way you would do things?

3. What differences in personality and style have you seen with your team or co-workers? How have you been able to work around these differences to minister to one another?

Chapter 35: What Will People Think?

1. What is expected of a good wife and mother in your host culture? How many of these expectations do you think you can meet?

2. Where do local values conflict with the cultural values you grew up with? Where do they conflict with biblical values?

3. Share some of your experiences trying to make decisions about what expectations you will strive to meet and which ones to let slide.

Chapter 36: The Comparison Trap

1. What are the most debated dos and don'ts concerning the lifestyle decisions in your host culture? Which ones do you think are the most important?

2. Do you struggle with guilt and indecision over some of these issues?

3. What could help you avoid falling into the comparison trap?

Chapter 37: An Answer to My Prayers

1. Have you ever lived with a local friend or had them live with you? Compare your experience to Catherine's (see also Jennifer's in chapter 16, "An Abundance of Friendships" and Vivian's in chapter 18, "A Troubled Believer").

2. Catherine gives advice for those who would have a local friend live in their house. With what would you agree or disagree? Is there anything you would add if you were advising a teammate?

3. Compare and contrast the advantages of having a roommate like Deborah and a more traditional house helper who just comes during the day. Would you be more open to one or the other?

Chapter 38: Hiring a House Helper

1. Share your attitudes about hiring house help. What do you see as the costs and benefits? What would you find confusing or intimidating?

2. If you have hired a house helper, share stories about how you set expectations and how things worked out.

3. What do you think of Laura's interpretation of Proverbs 31? Can you think of any other biblical principles that apply to this issue?

Chapter 39: Help with House Help

1. If you have had house helpers, share some of the things you have learned from them.

2. What do you think of Catherine's recommendation that new workers avoid getting their own houses? (See also chapter 33, "Choosing Where to Live.")

3. Share some of your own tips for managing employees. Are there things from Catherine's list you think are more or less important?

Part 5:
Singleness and Marriage

Living the Life God Gives You

40 Life and Leadership as a Single Woman

Ann,* an American woman in her late thirties, has been working in Southeast Asia for seven years. Although her ministry has gone through significant changes, for the first five years she lived among the Muslims she was trying to reach and was able to spend most of her time building relationships and ministering to people one-on-one.

"I expected singleness to be a problem, but in certain realms it has been a huge advantage," explains Ann. The freedom and flexibility she has to invest in studying the language and making friends is greater than that of many of the married people in her field of ministry. "The amount of time I have had to develop family-like relationships may be one of the huge differences between being married and single."

Many people in her home country assume women in a Muslim community, whether they are married or single, must be second-class citizens. Ann had some fears about this as well. Maybe nobody would listen to her or take her seriously. Maybe she would be restricted to the world of women and have to give up all contact with men and people in the professional world. Ann knows many women share her fears and cringe at the thought of a life reduced to cooking, clothes, kids, and gossip. "But that is not true with our people group. The women have a lot of input." As a working woman teaching English, Ann had more freedom than her teammates staying home with children. "And you can have significant relationships with men. We don't have them in our houses, but you can have a professional relationship and talk about significant issues."

* For more about Ann, see chapter 17. Choosing Your Friendships and 29. Taking a Backseat to Local Believers.

Proving Her Purity

As a single woman, she did have to prove herself in one sense: she had to demonstrate that she had high moral standards, especially sexually. "Even when I was living with another woman, there were assumptions for quite a long period that we had men hiding in the back room!" says Ann. "They found it so hard to believe that women our age could live a pure lifestyle. It doesn't make sense to them." Ann says it took eight months before she felt the suspicions had been dispelled. "The neighbors watched, but they *never* saw men going in." Ann and her housemate did not let their example speak for itself, though, but took initiative to help others understand. They had to be willing to talk about their lives, schedules, standards, and relationships in a way that was open so the neighbors would know they were living above reproach.

Although it may seem that proving their sexual morality is more of an issue for single women than any other part of the mission community, single men and married couples face some of the same challenges. In some Muslim societies, adultery is not uncommon. In most, westerners are believed to be sexually loose. After all, westerners do not have the forces of Islam to teach and reinforce their good behavior. Those who live far from their homes and families may seem particularly vulnerable to temptation. Peace Corp workers, businessmen, tourists, and other foreigners in the host country may demonstrate sexual immorality and give all westerners a bad name. American movies and television shows reinforce this. So, says Ann, "We had to be above board and not give the appearance of evil, but that is true for the married people as well."

Spared the Challenges Families Face

Although Ann is eager to see more married people and families come minister in her part of Southeast Asia, she recognizes they have great challenges she doesn't share. The leaders of the first team she was part of had several children. "They never got settled," Ann says sadly. Finding people to help them learn the language, setting up a way of life that worked for

Singleness and Marriage

their family, and figuring out how to socialize and educate their children held great challenges—challenges Ann and other singles did not face. Solving the problems they faced, Ann says, took a significant amount of time. "In certain ways, they never grasped the language to an adequate level. That led significantly to them leaving the field.

"In our area we have few options for education. You can send your kids to a boarding school but that is so expensive, and then you are away from the kids. Homeschooling was not a good option for our team; it just was not right. At the time, there was one family with young kids, just one family, and no other foreigners with children in the whole city. There was nobody they could ask for help or talk to about milestones in their child's life." Ann could listen, sympathize, and provide some help and company, but she was not going through the same things. "That would be true serving any people group on our island. The lack of a network is extremely hard. For the most part, the people making it and thriving in our field, to this day, are people who don't have kids. It's just really hard. In five years maybe things will be different."

Pausing to think, Ann mentions two families working in her part of the country who have kids and are doing well. She does not want to discourage others who would come, just to caution them about the challenges they may encounter. "It takes commitment, and a gift for homeschooling or a creativity to pursue other options." Families can make it in these situations, but they have to count the cost and be prepared for what they will face.

Running into Walls

Although she has seen great advantages in being single, Ann has also run into some problems, especially after she had to leave her direct church-planting ministry and invest instead in a strategy of training believers in a nearby culture to reach out to her focus people group. "I have found it to be much more difficult working with the church," she admits. "Before, I enjoyed being with the women more, but now we are working to train Southeast Asians."

For some time Ann was the leader and only foreigner involved in the training ministry, and then her status as a single woman became more of an issue. "It put me into positions where I was working with men. It simply had to happen. It was hard on them," she says. She could not go out for coffee or socialize freely with the men she was training, not like she could if she were a man. "They never said anything, but I know it was constantly on their minds," says Ann. They must have known other believers who were discipled by men who could be their buddies as well as their ministry consultants.

After more than two years of training nationals, Ann ran into a situation that revealed additional gender dynamics of which she had previously been unaware. "A strong conflict arose. I got angry with the national director of the Southeast Asian organization my team works with. He made a decision that I just felt was unwise. I questioned his actions in a culturally inappropriate way. I knew I'd acted out of the flesh and was in the wrong. But the offense he took was not that. It was another issue altogether: I had confronted him in front of his wife, and that mortified him. I now realize I may have damaged our relationship for a long time. And he let me know that as a single female, I have no right and no forum to criticize him at all. It doesn't matter how wrong he is. Two and a half years I have been doing this, a single female working with married men, and these things took that long to come out.

"Both status and marriage are quite important, almost more in working with Christian leaders than other kinds of people. Somehow with Muslims, our American-ness got us further. The local Christians may think, 'If you are a Christian, you should be like us.' So I've really bashed my head against a number of walls. I haven't been heard. I've been assumed not to be able to do something. Or they don't give me information; I'm kept outside. Our new team leader, Alex, has been in Southeast Asia for just over a year and in town only two months. And for him, it's different. He's got strong Christian leaders paying attention to every word he says. I have said the same things forty times, but he comes in and they listen! He's an older, married, pastor-type. And he fits right in."

Women in Mission Leadership

Ann's organization has some single team leaders, and some of them are single women. "The organization is quite empowering of women," says Ann. "The only thing they ever said is that it might be easier to recruit a team if you have a married couple, so married couples who want to join will feel that their needs will be met. I've felt empowered and encouraged by the organization, even if there are certain buddy-buddy relationships I'm left out of. Male team leaders may not feel as comfortable interacting with women team leaders as they do with other men."

It's still relatively rare for women, single or married, to lead field ministry, although quite a few of the married women function as co-leaders with their husbands. One of her organization's church-planting teams led by a single woman ran into problems over it, says Ann. "There was a guy who wanted to join the team and his home church would not let him because of their doctrine about women in leadership." Ann is not sure how the conflict was resolved.

Missions was once a man's world, but this has not been the case since more than one hundred years ago when, for the first time, women on the mission field outnumbered men. In Southeast Asia, and in Ann's sending agency, the imbalance continues. "There happen to be more single women missionaries than families in our city at this time. The realities are that there are more single women on the field, and often they end up lasting longer on the field because families go home for education or whatever. So I think we'll see more single team leaders and more women team leaders in the future. It was a positive experience for me, and it can be for others, but there are definite limitations."

41 Who Will Listen to a Single Woman?

Although sometimes she wonders what kind of influence she, a young single woman, can have in ministering to Muslims, Isabelle* has discovered her single status is not as much of a barrier as one might expect. Certainly being single "sticks out." She is different from other girls her age, particularly in the Central Asian country where she lives. However, as she explains, "I don't know if this would be true in other countries, but it's not always a question of being older, married, or having kids. I have been able to teach older women because they see that I have a gift for teaching."

People see that her ability is a sign of God's touch on her life. The same pattern shows up in the folk religion of the region. "There are eighteen or nineteen year old girls who are seen as having spiritual power," Isabelle explains. "People listen to them." As she has become fluent in the local language, she has seen more and more opportunities to minister to older women.

"There are definitely areas I can't speak to, like the marriage issues. When they have issues with their husbands, I don't quite understand. I have a feeling if I were married, they would talk to me more about those things. Now it's, 'Oh right, you don't understand because you're not married yet.' I am kind of glad I don't need to speak into sexual issues," Isabelle admits. "Probably the same would be true about parenting and issues with kids, except that I'm a teacher, and that brings me respect."

The local believers are even more willing to listen to those whom they believe to have wisdom or a special spiritual gift. "Hope, one of the believing girls from the village, was staying

---

* For more about Isabelle, see chapter 2. Cultural Immersion, 11. Looking Forward to Going Back, and 53. One-Room Schoolhouse.

with me. She made friends with the woman downstairs who has two kids and struggles with depression. This woman opened up to Hope. They talked a lot, and the woman took to heart Hope's advice based on the word of God."

Still, Is Singleness a Barrier to Ministry?

Would people listen to Isabelle more easily if she were married and had children? Likely they would. "My guess is that a woman with a husband and kids would have a voice that I don't," she says. Her married teammates still have hurdles to overcome in identification, though. Foreign women do not face all the same struggles that the locals do. Locals know this and point it out. They might say, "Your husband is so much nicer. He is involved at home and helps with the kids, and you don't have a mother-in-law you have to live with, so maybe you don't understand!"

In fact, one of Isabelle's friends is eager to marry a foreigner if she can meet a nice one on the Internet. She is separated from a husband who neglected her and she sees how kind-hearted the men on Isabelle's team are. She thinks they are better husbands than Central Asians are and that it is because they are American. This is a testimony to the work of the Holy Spirit in the lives of Isabelle's teammates, but it also shows that Central Asians still have trouble relating to them. Whether a missionary woman is married or single, her foreignness may place her in a separate category.

Answering Questions

It's helpful to think through the advantages and disadvantages that different people face in ministry, but in the end, God calls different kinds of people to missions and all of them need to obey him in that. "Think through who you are as a person, married or single, and what things characterize your life. How might God use those things? Think about why you are who you are, and have good answers for that. People came to Jesus with questions, and he responded. It's a natural way to do evangelism. The question 'Why are you single?' is one you can do many things with!

"One approach is to say, 'I am not married yet, but I trust in

God. He's going to bring the right person into my life, because he is sovereign and has it under control.'" In Isabelle's host culture, people don't want to be single or live alone because they are afraid of evil spirits. Isabelle, who has her own apartment, answers their questions about this with compassion but uses the conversation to point to God. "I can say, 'Well, I've lived at peace and never had a problem with the spirits. I've lived in peace and God has protected me.'"

Pointing People to God

Isabelle looks for other situations that she can turn into evangelism opportunities. She makes decisions about how she lives that demonstrate integrity rather than convenience, such as choosing not to tell lies. She is also careful not to pay bribes.

"There was a man who came to my door saying he was collecting for the electricity bill. I had lived there two years by then, so he said it was going to be $200. However, if I wanted to just give him $50, he would take care of it for me. 'Like a bribe you mean?' I said, 'Because I don't pay bribes.' My neighbor across the hall had been listening. 'Come on, things don't work that way here! Just pay the man!' she insisted. 'I want to honor God, and if $200 is what I owe, God will provide the money. I don't want to get off if that's what I owe,' I explained."

"What are you doing!" wailed the neighbor, wondering about this stubborn young woman who seemed to be forgetting everything they had taught her about how things work in Central Asia.

However, when Isabelle asked a trusted local friend for help, he went to the electric company and discovered that she only owed $24 for the two years. "I was able to tell the neighbors that. Even my adopted Central Asian family heard the story." They could see Isabelle's integrity in an ambiguous situation. "They tend to be very pragmatic people, so they notice things like that!"

Going along with the culture or swimming against its currents, Isabelle can use her situation to point her Central Asian friends to God. She cannot change who she is. Instead, she can minister from the midst of her circumstances.

42

Even a Healthy Marriage . . .

Before coming to the field, Vivian* knew the importance of a healthy marriage. A bad marriage could easily fall apart under the stresses of living in another culture. She didn't realize, though, how much a healthy marriage would experience stress. Now, she sees marriage stress as an inevitable part of cross-cultural life—especially in the beginning.

Friends and teammates have been experiencing many of the same emotions she and Trent did when they first came to Central Asia. "You are both adjusting to this culture and both experiencing culture stress," Vivian explains. "Sometimes you balance each other out, but it does come to a point where you are both stressed out emotionally, at the same time! You don't have any extra emotional energy for the other person. You may *both* be quite needy and vulnerable emotionally. So what do you do when you feel needy and the other person has nothing to give to you?"

Trusting Your Husband to Care for You

Westerners who are trying to live in and identify with a more traditional segment of their host culture, as Trent and Vivian are, may experience another stress on their marriages. "You come into a culture where women are not regarded very highly, and men are the kings. Because of the distance between men and women, I had this unspoken fear that it would affect Trent, and our marriage!" In other words, Vivian could picture her life becoming more and more separate from her husband's as he attempted to identify

---

* For more about Vivian, see chapter 1. Pajamas in Perspective, 7. Why Moms Should Learn the Language, 15. Bringing the Gospel of Peace, 18. A Troubled Believer, 20. Jesus in the Hospital Ward, 23. Available in the Busiest Season, and 53. One-Room Schoolhouse.

with and build relationships with men who had little interest in their wives' lives. "What was that going to do to our relationship? Was he going to abandon me or stop valuing our relationship in order to be more local? Will he stop listening to what I say? My teammate and I both thought about this. 'When local men don't care much for their wives, can we trust our husbands to still care for us?'"

Vivian needed reassurance of her husband's love and respect. "I went through the first eighteen months wondering what was going to happen here. Seeing that he still listened to me and respected me eased that fear, and we talked about it along the way."

Trent and Vivian did accommodate the patterns of the local culture in their marriage in some ways; rather than spending evenings with his wife, as would be their preference, Trent recognized that these were key times to spend talking on the street with neighborhood men. However, he arranged to spend more time with Vivian in the afternoons. So while they were not always able to spend as much time together as they liked, especially as their family grew, each year they have found ways to make get time together.

"Most men I know are also concerned about these things, but I have to say, I think I felt these issues more than Trent did. There were more issues having to do with me!"

In addition to learning how to keep her marriage healthy in her new context, Vivian was still learning how to be a mother. In this, especially, she felt the cost of leaving her support network behind. Now she wonders why, in addition to preparing to be a missionary overseas, she never thought to prepare to be a mom overseas. Some of the most practical problems she faced never came up in seminary or any pre-field orientation.

"I had questions like, 'What do I do with a screaming baby?' I needed a mom to talk to! Many of the hard things were ones I'd feel even in the States, but here I was kind of doing two adjustments at the same time: to the field and to motherhood. I didn't have the support in the motherhood adjustment that I'd have back home."

Helping Others Find Solutions

Some of Trent and Vivian's younger teammates have struggled with the same issues in their marriages: fear of losing the trust and intimacy, frustration over finding time to spend with each other, an inability to meet one another's needs, and adjusting to parenthood. Recently, the young couples on Vivian's team started gathering to share concerns and ideas. One team member invited an older couple with counseling experience to come from her home country and do a seminar on marriage issues for young couples on the field. When the "experts" had to cancel their trip at the last moment, the young couples got together anyway. Simply sharing their fears and questions with one another strengthened their marriages and helped them know they were not alone.

After two team members decided to marry, Trent and Vivian helped them work through basic issues. "We wrestled through some of these things with Maryanne and James before their marriage," says Vivian. "James was really concerned. And it was hard for him: here he was newly married, and he wanted to hold his wife's hand when they walked down the street." In Central Asia, men and women do not show affection to one another in public. Husbands and wives would not have anything like a "date" either, or even understand the concept. Maryanne and James had to find creative ways to quality time together and express their love for one another, just as Trent and Vivian had. "James and Maryanne had 'date nights' like this: they would lock their door and turn off all the lights and sit in their central room by candlelight, not answering the door or the phone, and have their date in the dark and quiet. You simply have to learn to adjust."

43 Allowing Your Marriage to Change

Like many westerners living cross-culturally, Laura* and her husband try to adapt to their host culture when they are around local friends. Without making some changes, Daniel and Laura would not be able to win the respect of their friends and neighbors, share the gospel, and speak into the lives of local believers.

But acting like a local has become more than a role for Laura. She can't be one person on the street and another when she's in her own home. For one thing, her local friends are often inside her house. For another, she's learned that culture seeps in further than one's skin. Even after just three years in Central Asia, she says, "I find I am becoming two people." The old patterns are still there, but she's developed new ways to live her life, ways that seem best for this context and this season of ministry. All this is affecting and reflected in her marriage, a fact Laura has learned to accept.

Adapting Your Marriage

Husbands and wives in Laura's host culture do not have the same expectation for time together that she was raised with. So, even though she may plan an evening with her husband, it may not happen. "I may think during the day, 'I'm just going to talk to Daniel tonight,' and then one of his friends will drop in. So Daniel is in the guest room with his friend, and I'm skirting between the kitchen and the bedroom; I am not spending time with the guest, much less my husband!" Laura and Daniel still find ways to spend time alone together and try to schedule it regularly, but their plans to do so—like any other plans they make—are subject to change.

In accordance with local expectations, Laura and Daniel are

---

* For more about Laura, see chapter 6. Marrying In and 38. Hiring a House Helper.

Singleness and Marriage

careful not to be physically affectionate in front of their friends or to talk to each other in ways they might in their home culture. "If he wants me to do something he should be kind and respectful, but he says, 'Do it.' However, I have to use honorific language and speak to him more gently: 'Please, if possible, could you . . . ?'" She tries to avoid teasing or joking with her husband in front of others, as well, and refers to him as her local friends speak of their husbands, with a term that might translate, "my master."

Laura still wonders if her husband is subconsciously taking on more of his friends' attitudes toward women than he intends. It's hard to say, because they have never been in breadwinner-housewife roles in a Western context. "I think Daniel acts a lot more independently of me than he would in the West," she says. "He's less likely to ring me to tell me he'll be late, for example. I don't think it's a conscious thing. He's just around locals all the time, and why would they tell their wives where they are going? For big things, like when someone asks him for money, he knows he can't lend without talking with me."

Roles and Responsibilities

Daniel, a kind and quiet man who likes to serve, would be happy to jump up and fill the teakettle or bring in food from the kitchen when they have guests. But Laura knows the culture expects her to take care of these responsibilities, so she tries to anticipate them. She recently hired a house helper, which should make a difference. For now, Laura is often exhausted by the social gatherings in their home, but she doesn't think she should accept her husband's help in most cases.

The birth of their first child has added a new wrinkle to the question of what marriage looks and feels like. Even more so than it would be in the West, caring for baby Grace is primarily Laura's responsibility. Daniel loves to play with her and cheerfully helps whenever he can. He comes home to watch Grace when Laura has language lessons. But for other activities, Laura must take Grace along or make other arrangements. When Daniel meets with a friend, he doesn't have to think about these things; Laura is always there to watch Grace and host Daniel's guests. When they have more children, the need for this division in roles might become more obvious and necessary. At this point, it still feels a bit awkward to Laura and something like a sacrifice.

Laura sometimes wonders if it is worth it. She is encouraged that friends and neighbors seem to appreciate her hard work. The mother of one of Daniel's friends told Laura that her son sees Laura as "the perfect wife." While Laura strives to be a dutiful housewife, she knows some women who have other roles. Her friend Jennifer has a wonderful ministry leading people to the Lord. "She is the leading evangelist in her city; the whole team says that. It probably doesn't worry anybody that she isn't a stereotypical housewife," says Laura. "She's still a good wife. She makes sure everyone can see how much she honors and respects her husband." Olivia, one of Jennifer's local friends, says it was seeing Jennifer and Robert's marriage that brought her to Christ. Laura admires that and aspires to have that kind of influence. It may just take time.

Taking Breaks

When Laura and Daniel take a break and leave the conservative city where they live, their former patterns surface again; they are able to "be themselves." Vacations in Western countries do much to refresh their marriage. Even a trip to the capital can be a welcome break, although it is more difficult for them since Grace was born. Laura likes the more casual nature of their relationship in such settings. "We relate more playfully, teasing, and we have more fun. It can be like a mini-honeymoon. We can hold hands in public and be silly!

"Then, coming back, I go through a day or two of mourning and recalibrating. I feel a little hurt, but I have to realize that Daniel is not mad at me or trying to be distant. He's just slipping into our local pattern. I may be sort of mean and nasty for a day or so after we get back, because Daniel stops relating to me like a westerner and starts relating more like a local. Your range of what is normal has to change. You lose some of it."

Appreciating the Local Patterns

Laura is grateful for her local friends, especially the younger ones who do not seem to have rigid expectations for her and her marriage. This helps her relax and keeps her from becoming bitter about the choices she is making or losing hope for local marriages. "Some local couples we know are less traditional. With them we can be more natural in the way we relate," she explains.

Among the local believers, Laura thinks of one couple who seem to have a strong marriage that both honors Christ and reflects the local culture. "Jimmy and Irene are a really traditional couple in some ways. When they talk to each other, they have no physical contact, for example. But the way they look at each other and the way they speak, you feel like they really love each other. They have a strong marriage, even though it looks different than what we would choose for ourselves. I like their marriage. I feel comfortable around it; one of them is not above and one below. I can joke around with them, too." Just because Laura and Daniel have a strong friendship with Jimmy and Irene does not mean they can relax their sometimes-stilted efforts to follow these local patterns. "I should still be careful about how much I joke with Daniel in front of them," says Laura, still learning to discern what is appropriate.

44 A Separate Ministry from Her Husband

In more than seven years on the field, Donna* has experienced missionary life as a single woman, as a married woman, and now as a mother of three. "I enjoyed being here single; I had a lot of freedom," she says, "But coming back as a married person I had so much more legitimacy. I had a role in the society that a single person doesn't have; I instantly had things in common with other women. There are things that are really different between my life and theirs, but I have ways to relate to people that I didn't before."

When she was single, Donna was never one who struggled with fears of never getting married and raising a family. But she did really want a partner in ministry with whom she could serve the Lord. But *partnership* means something different when ministering in places like the Central Asian country where Donna serves. "Being in a Muslim country—if I had thought this through I would have known—it's not what I expected. Yes, we are both really needed. But men and women really don't do things together. I've connected with some of the wives of guys he's worked with, and of course he needs me to host his guest!

"It's not the kind of partnership I was dreaming of," she admits. "Maybe one day we will be able to minister together, but for now it's not happening much."

Thinking through why things are the way they are has been helpful to Donna. When her husband, Kevin, goes out to meet with the men he disciples, Donna stays home with the kids. She has to remind herself that her ministry to the kids is a valuable aspect of their family's ministry. "I'm the parent for them that

---

* For more about Donna, see chapter 28. What God Has Not Promised, 35. What Will People Think? and 48. Can My Kids Learn This Language?

night; I'm there for them in a way that they don't feel lost. You can just pass the time, or you can invest in them. I invest in the kids so that Kevin can minister to someone."

In addition, Donna knows that if the local men are changed, the local women will be blessed as well. That doesn't mean that the women's ministry will go on without someone specifically ministering to women, but it helps her accept the limitations she is under for the time being. Several believing men in the country where Donna lives are regularly approached by women who want to know what makes them different! One of the things that God has used to draw women to the faith is seeing men's lives changed.

Learning a New Take on Teamwork

Donna would like to minister to the wives of her husband's friends, but she has to be practical. "If I go along, we have to bring the three kids. That would make four adults and maybe seven kids in two rooms! No ministry will go on. So we can visit, but I know if I go it doesn't mean I can work with that woman. So there was a kind of adjustment in my thinking."

Even when they have couples visit their own house, Donna's hands are somewhat tied. This can be frustrating at times: "If he sits and does nothing and I have to serve the food and take care of the kids, especially if the wife is as good a friend of mine as the husband is of Kevin's, yes, it's hard. Especially if one of the kids is having a bad night and Kevin has to engage with the guest and I can't get his help. Sometimes I am just disappointed."

Now her three little children are at a stage where they can play together quite well, but there was a time when she had two babies to feed and put to bed as well as a toddler; so if guests came at 7:00, she would have no time for them. "I tried to have guests on days my house helper came so she could cook at least!" she says.

Hosting guests is essential to ministry in this culture, so her inability to sit and talk tends to mean Donna is being a good hostess, not a bad one. She's had to find other ways to get that kind of interaction, that's all. Instead of ministering as a family, Donna meets with her ministry contacts one on one.

 A Separate Ministry from Her Husband

Even then, figuring out what to do with her kids is a challenge. "Meetings happen when they happen. One girl I work with now has a two-and-a-half-year-old. We talk and make it work, but you are always being interrupted," explains Donna. "That's just part of discipleship here. It has to look different, to be different."

Because of the lifestyle in their city, their ministry brings a lot of phone calls and visits, but not many people just show up at the door. However, when they do, Kevin and Donna have learned subtle ways to communicate in front of guests. If Donna really needs help, she can let her husband know. "It's good if you both know what it means when one of you gives the other a certain look!" she says with a laugh.

Donna also appreciates how good her husband is at pitching in with kids and chores. "It's understood that I will be more engaged with the kids than he will, and that's just the way it needs to be. But he's really good about seeing we have a family night every week, a time when he is really engaged with the family."

Discussion Questions for Part 5

Chapter 40: Life and Leadership as a Single Woman

1. What do you see as the advantages of singleness in ministry? To what extent do you think Ann's experience would be the same in other cultures you know?

2. Have you ever had to "prove" your sexual purity? What rules and expectations was it important for you to follow?

3. How would you feel about having a female team leader? What do you think would help women in these positions do well?

Chapter 41: Who Will Listen to a Single Woman?

1. Isabelle lives in a culture where even people of low status may be listened to if others sense they have a special gift. Do you think this would work in the culture where you serve? Have you seen any models of younger or unmarried women having influence?

2. How would you answer questions from locals about being single or not having children? What advice have you heard from other women in those situations?

3. Are there other ways your "different-ness" might be an opportunity to point people to Christ?

Chapter 42: Even a Healthy Marriage . . .

1. What stresses have you faced in your marriage while living cross-culturally? Which of these stresses might you face anywhere?

2. How have you experienced and responded to dynamics like the ones Vivian describes?

Chapter 43. Allowing Your Marriage to Change

1. How much does your host culture value friendship and affection between husbands and wives? What pressures might this put on a more Western marriage? How do you respond?

2. To what extent do you think you can or should let your marriage change? Can you be "two different people" like Laura describes? How do you feel about Laura's approach?

Chapter 44. A Separate Ministry from Her Husband

1. If you are married, to what extent are you and your husband able to do ministry together? How does this align with your hopes and expectations?

2. In what ways can you support your husband in his ministry to men? In what ways can your husband support you in ministry to women?

3. How do you respond when ministry and family needs seem to pull you in two different directions?

Part 6:
Parenting

Family Issues, Choices, and Models

45   In This as a Family

When their daughters, Molly and Cassie, were twelve and ten, Kathleen[*] and her husband, Peter, moved from their home in Canada to a small Muslim city in Central Asia to become missionaries. This was an important decision for their family, and as parents of precocious daughters, Kathleen and Peter wanted their daughters to have an active voice in this decision. When teammates Matthew and Rebecca visited their church on furlough, they invited Kathleen's family to come see their work. "At the time we were seriously considering options both here in Central Asia and in North India. Half the family thought we should go to India, and half thought we should come here to Central Asia.

"So," explains Kathleen, "we delayed our coming for four months until we were at a point where we knew God had spoken to all *four* of us about coming here. We could not just bring them along with us as if they were babies. It wasn't like God was calling us to be the missionaries and these were only the kids we have with us. We are not two missionaries and two MKs; we are four missionaries.

"Working through the decision to come as a family has really helped. When hard times come, which they do, they hit us at different times and in different ways. We remind each other, 'We made this decision together.' This has made us stronger, and the girls don't resent us as parents."

Kathleen's family has had more time together overseas than they did back home. In Canada Kathleen stayed home and homeschooled the girls, while Peter worked a professional job and had a long commute. Now Peter walks five minutes to work and has lunch and dinner with his family, and he even helps with the homeschooling. Kathleen spends much of her time at home, but

---

[*] For more about Kathleen, see chapter 8. Misadventures in Language Learning.

now she too has a desk job, working for their team's development company.

"I do like the fact that we live much more 'as a family.' People in Canada really live in isolation, in comparison. We interact more with each other, and with our neighbors."

Relationships under Pressure

Even if everyone is in it together, coming to the field can still put a lot of pressure on a family. Kathleen and Peter's first year on the field has not been easy. "Our relationships have been under great strain, relationally, emotionally, and spiritually," says Kathleen. "Not just for us as husband and wife, but between children and parents. Generally our girls have really enjoyed being sisters, but here they find their patience running short. It's often due to culture and language fatigue, and not having many good friends they can play with easily."

Peter and Kathleen had been married many years before they became missionaries, which helped them to weather the strains of relocation, but the move still put a lot of strain on their relationship. "Sometimes we are just plodding along and don't have the energy to work on our marriage. Last fall we were getting to the point where we were not dealing with each other in healthy ways. Peter had a lot of anger, and I was trying to manipulate him into doing things. Finally we went to our team leaders about it."

As it turned out, everyone on their team had gone through similar struggles in their marriages—taking on, in fact, many of the local, less-than-healthy patterns for relationships between husbands and wives. Somehow, under pressure, Kathleen and Peter had picked up the same tendencies. As they saw what was happening, they gained the tools to understand and fight these negative patterns. "It has not been easy, but we survived," says Kathleen simply.

Language Learning for Older Kids

Kathleen and Peter's commitment to being a "family of missionaries" may have put their girls under more pressure than some missionary kids face, but it has also had great rewards.

"We believe that language learning and culture adaptation are as important for our kids as for us," says Kathleen. "Many families we meet don't have this approach." The kids in some families she knows seem to live in a Western bubble, in a different culture than their parents. Sometimes these kids may be oblivious to what is culturally appropriate in one setting or another. If they don't understand the language and culture or keep schedules similar to those of other kids in the community, they cannot play with their neighbors and only spend time with other Western children. "We see that and know it won't work for our family," explains Kathleen.

Molly and Cassie are still schooled in English and at home, but it has taken time to find age-appropriate ways for them to learn the local language. Younger children are often able to learn the language on the street or in school. Molly and Cassie do learn some from their local friends, but at this age they need a little more structure for learning the language. The girls began learning the language by taking a course in the capital with their parents.

"We are so proud of them. It's designed for adults, and they did it all, including all the homework," says Kathleen with evident pleasure. "We had class every morning, and they did their homework along with us every afternoon. Our family was really in it together, learning and studying together. It was great."

After settling into the community where they would live long-term, the girls began studying with a young teacher they met. This woman, a believer, had a heart for worship and used local worship songs to teach the girls the local language. As a result, Molly and Cassie know more Christian songs in the local language than most of the adults on their team. Now the girls study with their father's teacher who enjoys playing language games with them. She prepares lessons and comes to their house. During each session they learn half a dozen or more new words, practice their new words in sentences, and write about assigned topics. It can be too much at times: the girls have language lessons three times a week on top of their regular schoolwork. So they do get tired. When it is time for a vacation, they need it as much as their parents.

Making Friends

Although learning the local language has helped, Kathleen's daughters have had more trouble finding local playmates than they expected. This is partly because, for one reason or another, the family has lived in seven different houses in a year. While this has helped their family make a variety of friends, understand the different parts of the city, and know what type of living situation will work for them, it has kept everyone from putting down roots and building solid friendships.

Molly and Cassie's experience has varied from one neighborhood to the next. The girls are committed to honoring the local culture, but their young friends can be less forgiving of differences and struggles than adults might be. "In the first neighborhood we lived in," explains Kathleen, "people were very antagonistic to us as Christians. They would say things like, 'Are you a Christian?' and the girls would answer carefully, 'We believe in the one God and follow Jesus the Messiah.' Then the neighborhood kids would say, 'Christians are bad! Muslims are good!' In the second neighborhood, the kids just wanted to play with the girls' toys and wouldn't return them, and they showed little interest in relationships."

In another place the family stayed, Kathleen's girls had a better experience. There were half a dozen girls their age in the neighborhood, girls who were kind, sweet, and caring. "One day they called for Molly, but she was not feeling well so couldn't come out and play. Not long after, a group of nine girls came knocking, bringing fruit and bread and ice cream. They had come to pay respect to the sick person! There really are nice girls in this city! But this was the girls' first experience like that after being here for a year," says Kathleen. They were only in that neighborhood for a few weeks, house-sitting for a teammate. Mollie and Cassie were not able to build long-term relationships there, but it gave them hope that it could happen again.

Looking Ahead

As her daughters enter their teens, Kathleen expects the issues they face to change. At twelve, Molly is at the age when many local girls are starting to take more responsibility in the house and are less available to come out and play, so many of the girls she meets and plays with are younger than she is. Also, she is too old to wear the ready-made children's clothes available at the bazaar, and will need to adjust to dressing and behaving as a young lady.

As a more conservative Muslim country nearby has begun to open up, Peter has visited to investigate opportunities to serve and support work there. Like many workers in the region, he and Kathleen wonder if God might someday call them to embrace the new opportunities in that needy country. However, it would be challenging to take daughters on the brink of maturity into such a setting.

Meanwhile, Kathleen anticipates the day when her family will need to return to their home country. "We feel confident we can provide what the girls need until Molly is nearly done with high school," she explains. "That will give us a good five years here. Then we need to head back home for a few years to settle their schooling and get them started in university, if that's what they choose. After that, perhaps Peter and I can return to the field."

Whatever the timeline may be and wherever they choose to live, Kathleen believes they will make those decisions as they have made all the others, as a family.

46 On and Off the Field with Babies

It's been more than five years since Gwen* and her husband, Tom, came to Central Asia as church planters. Yet their five years have been punctuated by quite a few transitions—including leaving the field for the birth of each of their sons. These interruptions introduced new challenges to Gwen's life. A course in language-learning techniques got the young couple off to a good start, as did their mission agency's arrangement for them to spend nine months in full-time language study and immersion. "Then I taught at the language institute while my husband was doing a construction project," says Gwen. Gwen did not realize how much motherhood would change this. After a year and a half on the field, she got pregnant and they went home to the States to have the baby. When they returned as a family, Gwen found her life and ministry began to change.

"I haven't been able to get going really well with my language studies since then, and I don't have a language helper. With babies, language learning happens when you have time! The main person I communicate with in the local language is my house helper. She's a neighbor and a good friend. I can't get out much with young kids. Now, our older son is almost three and the baby is nine months old."

The Effects of a Long Furlough

Gwen has found that although having kids opens opportunities for her in relationships, there are significant personal costs. Many families like Gwen's will take a furlough of six months or so with the birth of each child. After spending time with family members and taking advantage of public-speaking opportunities,

*For more about Gwen, see chapter 49. Finding a Ministry through Parenting.

Parenting

the furlough may seem quite long without being restful. This may not be avoidable. Few missionary families in the country where Gwen lives see having their babies in a local hospital as a viable option. Some have the opportunity to go to nearby countries with more developed medical systems. Most, though, return to their home countries. Emotionally, it can be quite a comfort. Yet there is a cost as well.

"Our son Justin was just starting to talk when we left Central Asia and was speaking more of the local language than English, but in the eight months we were in the States to have the baby and our furlough, he forgot everything. When we came back in May, he did not even recognize our house! Friends here were offended when he did not know them. He had to completely re-learn the local language. We did not expect this at all. My friend Veronica tells us one of her kids went through the same thing at this age. 'It can take six months to get back to where they were,' she says. 'It's been four months so far.'" Now three-year-old Justin is starting to understand more of the language again. Although he cannot say very much, he can count in the local language and knows a handful of other words.

Because of the language barrier, Justin has also struggled with making friends in the neighborhood. "The first month after we came back, he wanted to play with the local kids, but he'd come in crying, saying, 'Mom, they are talking to me! I don't know what they are saying!' After a month or two of that he became more comfortable," says Gwen. "Now he is finally at a place where he can enjoy playing with them."

Balancing Demanding Roles

Like many women, Gwen struggles to be at peace with the balance between the needs of her family and children and her ministry. "My children are my priority, whatever else I have to give up. Part of me thinks if I'm still nursing, that's all I should do. But after this baby, we'll have another, and I don't want to *never* have a ministry. We had wanted four children, but now I'm not so sure," she admits. "I don't think I can go through being stuck at home so much with another baby.

"I'm an extrovert, and staying home so much has been the hardest thing. I am really depressed at the end of the day if I haven't gotten out, because I get my energy from being with people. If I can't even get out to have five-minute conversations, it's hard. We have a car, and I drive; I'd be stuck here otherwise. I can't get the stroller in a taxi, and it's a long walk to get a taxi anyway. For an hour in the afternoon we can jump in and go to a park or something, and that helps tremendously."

All of this may be harder for Gwen because she remembers what it was like before she had kids. In some ways she is still counting the cost of giving up that way of life. She was also a single missionary for five years before her marriage. Gwen does not get out much now, and she knows what she is missing. On the other hand, her years of ministry experience before the kids came along have given her a maturity that helps her be creative and flexible with the opportunities and limits she has now.

"Just in the past several weeks I've been able to work in discipling a gal we led to the Lord a few years ago; my husband will come and stay with the kids when they are napping so I can have a couple of hours to study with her. Yesterday she and I took our kids to a park together. So that gives me something, ministry-wise. My house helper wants to study the Word together this winter. I'm too busy now, but while the kids are napping, maybe we can do that. If I don't invest in her, who can?"

Gwen can also laugh about her circumstances and see how God uses the humblest things. "Right now the thing that works best is that my son loves dirt! There are always families in the neighborhood working on their houses, and they will have a big pile of dirt in front. He wants to play in it. So I take the baby, and he takes his dump trunk, and that's where we go. The kids come out, and then the ladies. This is the best interaction I can have now: we go play in the dirt! This is my life. I didn't think it would come to this, but it's actually a lot of fun."

Parenting ❀

47 Helping Your Kids Feel Heard

Catherine* has a busy ministry of hospitality. After seven years in Central Asia she's fairly fluent in the local language, so she doesn't spend much time in language study. A capable house helper does most of the cooking and cleaning. Her children are in a local school as well as a homeschooling program outside of the house. And, although she does not have children under her feet all the time, she still has quality family time with her husband and kids most evenings. In other words, Catherine has now reached an easier stage in the life of a missionary mom.

However, she still faces some of the most common challenges. For example, when she focuses on local relationships, her kids sometimes feel neglected. "Guests can come at any time of the day, and this can create jealousy for your kids. They see you focus on someone else. Even when you are busy with something, they still come to you to resolve things for them. When they were small I had to take them to the bathroom; now I have to settle their fights. You know, 'He's picking on me!'"

The Language of Attention

One thing Catherine has had to learn is how to respond to her children in the presence of local friends. The children speak and understand the local language well enough, so at first she did not switch to English to respond to their problems. Using the local language ought to work, she thought, and it would make her guests feel more at home. However, this did not seem to work with the kids. "I found if I said, 'Just a minute, Mommy is talking

---

* For more about Catherine, see chapter 26. Sickness, 37. An Answer to My Prayers, 39. Help with House Help, and 53. One-Room Schoolhouse.

 Helping Your Kids Feel Heard

now,' in the language my guests understood, it might not register with the kids. They had trouble understanding me!

"It seems funny that they can understand their teachers but not me! I've been told that children can go back and forth between languages, but if the person is matched to the wrong language, they don't understand. They don't feel I've given them my attention. So, I had to decide it was all right to speak to my child in English. If I'm uncomfortable doing that in front of a local friend, we can go into the other room."

Catherine also realized the way she responded to her children was sometimes sending them the wrong message. If she was talking to a guest and the kids wanted something, she would often tell them she was busy.

"Then I heard them using the expression, 'I'm busy,' with each other when they were tired or didn't want to do something. That's what they thought the expression meant! I realized they got that from me and have tried to change it. I've also tried to reduce interruptions by teaching them to touch my arm to get my attention. Not that they always do that," she says with a laugh, "but it has helped.

"Another way to help kids feel valued when a visitor comes is to let them be a part of the hosting process," says Catherine. "In Central Asia, when a visitor comes, at the very least, hot tea and bread is to be put out on a tablecloth in front of the guest. As soon as my kids were able to walk, I gave them bread or a dish of raisins, whatever they could carry, to take and set before the guest. This made them feel important and a part of the visit, not just pushed aside when someone came. Now that they are older (eight and ten), they know the routine and can do everything except pour the hot water while I am free to visit with the friend."

Daring to Discipline

Another issue she has faced is how to discipline her children when local friends are looking on. "Sometimes disciplinary action has to take place at that present time," says Catherine. "I don't want my kids thinking that they can get away with things just because a visitor is in our house—though that's what people in the local culture do. A naughty child is often appeased with sweets or given what he wants. If I'm at a local person's house, they usually have someone else around who can take the disruptive child away. The other thing they do is to just give them a piece of candy and say, 'Go!' Sometimes they will take the child into their lap and let them cuddle and sit quietly. Showing our friends that parents can be in charge (without getting angry) and that they can expect obedience from their children is a great way to model basic concepts of godly parenting."

During their first year on the field, the local family Dan and Catherine lived with was surprised by their parenting approach. "They were appalled when we sent one of the kids to stand in the corner as a punishment for something. After a while they realized the child was not damaged psychologically or health-wise by it, and that the child was usually better behaved as a result."

One-on-One Time

As long as kids get some special time talking with you face-to-face in the morning and at bedtime, Catherine suggests, they are happy to play or do other things when you have a guest and can't talk to them. They just need that specific attention.

She and her husband, Dan, also found that spending time together as a family is not the same as giving their kids individual time. Now they try to be sure each child is getting personal attention. Catherine's husband Dan has "tea times" with each of his children on a regular basis. "I hadn't realized how helpful it was until I did it," says Dan. "We had family times, but I didn't realize how important it was to give individual attention to each child." Just like adults, kids behave differently as a group than one-on-one. "As a group you relate to them one way; as individuals, you relate to them differently."

48 Can My Kids Learn This Language?

Donna* loves having three young children at home, but a year or two ago she started sending her oldest child to a local preschool in the hopes that this would help him be more comfortable in the community. She was to find that her ideals were no match for the circumstances.

One reason for this was that Donna's little boy Jeffrey hated the school and had to be forced to go. Donna knew she had to make another plan. She still thought that sending him out would be best in the long run, but she found another way to do it. A play group with the children of other missionaries and some local believers made a good in-between step until he was ready to go back to the school.

Now, her two youngest children have started school, so they all go the community preschool together. Things are better now than they were at first. "I still bring them home at lunch time, because the twins won't eat the food there," says Donna. "The teacher wants me to scold them for being picky and make them eat it, but you can only push your kids so far."

It can be hard for westerners to send their kids out of the house into a culture that may seem threatening and a school system where criticism flows more freely than affirmation. "You have got to find the right school and right teacher," says Donna.

Why would she push her children into these kinds of situations? "My biggest motivation for having the kids in the local preschool is for them to learn the language."

---

* For more about Donna, see chapter 28. What God Has Not Promised, 35. What Will People Think?, and 44. A Separate Ministry from Her Husband.

Parenting

Helping Kids to Be Comfortable at Home

Speaking only English, Donna's kids might do just fine socially. They live in city with a relatively large expatriate community. But, being the children of church planters, they live in a house where the local language is spoken at home more frequently than English is, especially when there are guests. Donna was not willing to make her home an English haven—though she does want it to be a haven for her kids. For that to happen, they need to have some ability in the local language.

"The older they get, the more important it is for me to see that they know what's going on in their home. So we wanted them to attend a local preschool and a year or two of regular school; whatever it takes."

When their oldest son was little, he loved guests. Then he started pulling back. Now, as Jeffrey understands more of the local language, he is more comfortable again. Donna is pleased. "That's my goal, that they be comfortable that this is their home."

She would also like her kids to feel comfortable in the homes of the family's local friends. Kevin and Donna usually take the children along when they go visiting. "Our friends know they are coming; it's part of the deal. My kids are still young, though; we haven't hit the 'I'm bored, I don't want to go!' thing yet. Usually, they find something to do and play with the other kids."

Helping Kids Learn

"I think it's good for our kids to learn a second language when they are little," says Donna. "So many kids don't." However, one of the assumptions she had was that kids could just pick up language on their own as long as they were around other kids speaking the language. "That's just not true. Some kids do, and some kids don't." Now, she wishes she had known it was okay to do something as "unnatural" as create a learning structure for her kids, instead of expecting them to pick it up.

"The whole thing is motivation. Jeffrey is very independent and introverted. He's not shy, but he only has so many social needs, and his brother and sister meet them. That may change later. Anyway, he didn't have a need or desire for the local language. Jeffrey was totally not motivated to talk to other people. Finally we found language helpers who play language games with him. I never told them to do it; they just thought it would help. It seems to be working. Another thing is that he is totally motivated by what 'Daddy' says. Kevin started asking him every night, 'What new word did you learn?' Kevin really plays this up, and it's been a huge thing for Jeffrey.

"Each step along the way, the Lord has provided the exact place that was right for our kids at that time. We just keep asking for that, for our next step." And, as Donna tells other workers who struggle to know how much to push their kids, "Keep praying."

49 Finding a Ministry through Parenting

Coming to the field without children, Tom and Gwen* were able to throw themselves into language and culture learning. They made friends and became part of a traditional community on the edge of their city. Before they had children, they built relationships and grew to love their new community. When Gwen became pregnant, she wondered how having children would change things.

"When I come back from the States with my baby," says Gwen, "suddenly he was not just my baby. He belonged to the neighborhood. I knew when I had a child, I wanted him to have the benefits of the community.

"Every day, or every other day at least, I'd have someone at the door asking to take him for a couple of hours. It was free babysitting! So whenever they came asking, I'd mentally check his schedule to see when he'd been fed and when he needed to rest. If it was a good time, I'd let them take him. It's nice for me, too!"

In her host culture, everyone pitches in to take care of children. "For example," says Gwen, "if you go to a party, everyone helps with the kids so the adults can sit. The child is out of your hands. They want you to sit and enjoy yourself and not think about your child."

But Gwen was a little naïve. Neighbors doted on her blond, blue-eyed boy and treated him as a very special person. Not surprisingly, he became a bit spoiled and demanding. Local friends also liked to give the foreign baby treats. "No matter what

---

* For more about Gwen, see chapter 46. On and Off the Field with Babies.

 Finding a Ministry through Parenting

I told them, he would come home with chocolate all over his face!" she says with dismay.

Other women in Gwen's situation have faced the same issues. Another woman in Gwen's host culture says she hesitates to take her baby out on the street very often because everyone she meets feels they have a right to kiss him soundly—and every little kid with a runny nose is sure to do so. Is it worth it, risking her baby's health to avoid offending the neighbors? Women who can "die to self" with their own comfort level may find it more difficult to put their children in uncomfortable or potentially dangerous situations.

Deciding to Pull Back

With some reluctance, Gwen and her husband came to the conclusion that they were not willing to raise their son the way the neighbors raised theirs. "I realized we would have to do something different. For example, we couldn't give in to the local pressure to keep him up until 11 p.m. and then take a three-hour nap."

Not all of her neighbors understood why Gwen drew back and no longer allowed them to spoil her little boy. "We had to make tough decisions that distanced us from people we were close to. I could have more freedom if I did things their way. But raising these kids is a responsibility God has given me; I form my kids' habits. If I let local ways take over, my kids will be like the local kids. And," she says with a sigh, "I can't have that, as terrible as it sounds to say so."

This decision was a tough one, but Gwen sees it paying off in her kids' character and development. Some of her local friends are impressed as well. "Our house helper, Kelly, is here three days a week, and she sees it. The ladies we are close to ask Kelly, 'How come Gwen never comes over to see us anymore?' but she tells them about our schedule and how well it works. 'You should see Gwen's kids sleep when she puts them down!'

"It helps having Kelly as an advocate. She tells them I am committed to my kids, and that is not something they are used to seeing."

Parenting

Modeling Good Parenting

Although she no longer lets the neighborhood raise her sons by committee, Gwen is starting to see ways her neighbors may benefit from the commitments she has made as a mom. "Something I'm feeling called to is the whole area of parenting. I'm seeing how God is opening doors: mothers are asking me how I did it. 'My child is throwing tantrums all the time,' they say. I'm wondering what God might be doing. This whole area is a huge hole: it's not the mom who cares for the kid, but whoever is at home."

Gwen has begun to see the dark side of local parenting practices. "The women do not feel responsible for doing what is best for their children." Many of these cultural differences result from placing a lower value on human life, says Gwen, who estimates that the older women on her street have had an average of four or five abortions. Abortion and abstinence are the only widely used forms of birth control. Without taking on that whole social issue, Gwen wonders, "How can we help people see that every child is a gift from God?"

When Gwen's closest local friend got married and was pregnant soon after the wedding, Gwen wondered what kind of mother Jenny would be. Just a few years into her marriage, Jenny had two babies, both premature and only a year apart. Like a typical young bride, Jenny lives with her husband's parents, and her mother-in-law makes most of the rules in the house, including how to care for and raise the new babies. "At first I thought the mother-in-law was keeping her from taking good care of them. Now I see that Jenny could take responsibility, but she just doesn't. Maybe I can help her learn."

50

The Perils
of Parenting
Preschoolers

Robert and Jennifer's two preschoolers race around the large, rambling house in a down-and-out-neighborhood of a small Central Asian city, dodging the baby's crib in the kitchen. Robert and Jennifer* came to the field seven years ago. This is the only home their kids have known. Helping them accept life in Central Asia has not been difficult. However, helping them learn the local language, make friends, and begin their education has taken Jennifer down some roads she did not expect.

"Last year we tried to send them to preschool to help them fit in," Jennifer says. "We searched the city for the best one; friends helped us find one with clean bathrooms and running water; the kids had their own bowl and spoon instead of sharing. They had all these nice toys, too. But it turned out the toys were just for show; the kids weren't allowed to play with them! They were not even allowed to run and around and play outside very much, because keeping an eye on them would be too much work for the staff."

The staff never read to the children or stimulated them in any way. Jennifer even gave the school a children's Bible in the local language, but they never read any of the stories to the children. Jennifer's kids only went three days a week for half a day, but it was always a struggle. "They were really good about it. They'd pray in the car on the way over there, 'Please help us like school; please let us have fun there!'"

After six or nine months in the local school, Jennifer gave up. "We really tried; our intention was to send the kids to local

---

* For more about Jennifer, see chapter 16. An Abundance of Friendships, 22. The Cost of Compassion, and 30. Suddenly Rich.

schools like some of our other friends in ministry, but our city is much smaller and there aren't good schools here."

Even though she pulled her kids out of the local school system, Jennifer still wants them to learn to speak the local language so they can participate in ministry and live well-adjusted lives in their host culture. So far the family's furloughs have been longer than they'd like. Robert and Jennifer are from different countries, and it seems to take at least six months to spend time with family in both places and catch up with supporters. They have also left Central Asia for the births of their children, which makes for longer or more frequent furloughs. A six-month furlough is not unusual for many missionaries, but Jennifer doesn't like it. It disrupts her ministry and affects the children's ability to retain the local language.

"Last year we ended up being gone for seven months, so the kids forgot everything! Now we have a teacher come for them three times a week. She makes it fun for them. Right now she is teaching them the alphabet. I'm not sure how useful it is since they can't read and write," says Jennifer with a laugh, "but she was so enthusiastic I let her try it."

Jennifer and Robert are also homeschooling their kids. They love that time to be with them and the chance to teach them their values. "For a long time I wondered what kind of mom I'd be," says Jennifer. "I wanted to have my passion for raising my kids to be even greater than my passion for the local people, and God has done that. I have a real vision for it now. I'm content to be at home.

"We have to homeschool, the way we see it, and we are glad. The kids love it: school means quality time with mom and dad. I think that's God's way of keeping us from being just ministry minded and losing touch with the kids.

"At the same time, God is so gracious to bring people to me for ministry. Neighbors come to my door in the afternoon with a need, and I get to pray and share the gospel. I love it that way. It's the grace of God and his mercy on my kids that we can be together and love it. I still disciple leaders' wives and share the gospel with friends, especially after the kids are in bed."

❧ The Perils of Parenting Preschoolers

Finding Friends for the Kids

Jennifer's kids usually play with one another. Being close in age, they always have a best friend handy. They also have some foreign friends. Finding local friends has been more difficult. "We're looking for a soccer team for little kids so Colin could join, if something like that exists."

Sometimes Jennifer's kids play with the children of local believers. Her house helper has a son the same age as Jennifer's, and the kids go to her house. Sometimes they spend the night with her when Jennifer and her husband have a "date night." It's fun for them and good for language practice. One of Jennifer's believing neighbors has a daughter who sometimes comes to the house to play, but Colin does not have a close friend among the local boys. "We used to know a great family he would play with every day, but they moved!" So Jennifer prays, "Lord, please help us find a nice boy Colin's age!"

The tough neighborhood in which Jennifer's family lives is not the best place to look for playmates. "There are drug addicts, alcoholics, and prostitutes in our neighborhood. Half their kids don't go to the school, and the school that's here is chaotic. The kids are always running around and yelling; cursing at each other and at their teachers. The boys who are Colin's age here usually play in the creek out front. But everyone puts their trash there, and it's full of sewage. We don't want our kids to play there and get sick.

"We chose this neighborhood ourselves; we really wanted to be here with the down-and-outs. But we don't want our kids to be eaten by wolves. We need to protect their minds, spirits, and bodies. The kids are not as much 'in the community' as we would hope, but they are basically happy. We believe that they will be healthy, secure kids, and that is more important than feeling local. For our family, it's the right thing."

What Does It Mean to Put Family First?

It's taken Robert and Jennifer some time to figure out how to put family first. Robert is in a position of leadership in the team

Parenting

and agency and has a lot of demands on his time, especially in the evenings. "We always said family is priority but were finding it wasn't true. We said our kids are not going to be the kind of MKs who think the locals are more important than they are. But as it happened, guests or crises would come and our family night was always put off!

"Now, Tuesday and Thursday nights are set in stone as family nights. All day Saturday is family time, too; we don't open the door or answer the phone. We have a date night every other week. Our team, the believers, and our neighbors know that now. They also know that Mondays and Wednesdays are totally open, and Sundays as well. If we have to do something else, we change things around to get family night in. This has made such a difference for the kids; they feel so much more settled.

"We hope to stay on the field as long as possible. We're committed to staying here until a church-planting movement is established, although we're willing to go back to North America for health or education, if it's needed, for however long. Our kids are our highest priority, even above our calling as missionaries. After watching a television special when we were in America, Colin has been praying for Afghanistan every night; maybe our family will be called there next. As a family, this work is a lifetime thing."

Room for Differences

Robert and Jennifer regret that their initial dreams for their kids to find neighborhood friends and attend local schools have not worked out, but they accept their situation and try to avoid guilt, defensiveness, and comparisons. Some friends and teammates do things differently.

A wise person once gave Jennifer a piece of advice. "'Two things you never judge a family on: how they use their finances and how they raise their kids.' This is tough on an international team!" admits Jennifer. Members of Robert and Jennifer's team come from several different home countries. "We've had to agree to disagree about some things about parenting. Women's identity, especially, is so wrapped up in their kids that there can be a huge fallout over issues like homeschooling and training children. I guess it's like that back home, too," she says.

51 Parenting Long Distance

For several years Lauren and her husband have been working in a Central Asian country as field leaders for their organization. They have two teenaged daughters, Leah and Ellen, now away at boarding school, and a younger son, Matthew, still at home. "There are pluses and minuses to the boarding school situation," says Lauren, who is British, but for her the advantages outweigh the disadvantages.

Before sending her kids to boarding school, Lauren had experience with some other options. When she first came to Central Asia, she gave homeschooling a try. "It's is not my cup of tea, though, and it's not a UK thing," says Lauren. The British school system does not lend itself easily to homeschooling. To do it well she would need to spend five or six hours a week in preparation, "plus do school from nine to twelve every morning, and language study and hosting in the afternoon. I can't multitask like that! Some people can."

Then her family relocated to a larger city that had an international school. "That was a relief. It's one reason why we have stayed in the city."

Even so, by the time Leah, their oldest, approached her teen years, Lauren was prepared to let her go back to England. Lauren feels that it is important for MKs to spend some part of their teenage years in their home country. "They need to learn to live in the normal world," says Lauren. Age eighteen is too late to begin learning about their own culture and how to cope with its pressures.

The Benefits of Boarding School

While boarding school is not for everyone, kids who go to boarding school often adapt better to their home culture than those

 Parenting Long Distance

who don't, says Lauren. "We want our kids to get to experience life and know what it's like to be a teen in the UK; otherwise it will be a shock when they hit college."

Many parents leave the field as their kids hit secondary school. Others send their kids home to live with friends or family and go school in their home country, or they find a good boarding school in another country. Lauren and her husband were able to send their daughters to a British boarding school. Not only is she confident that her kids will get a good education, Lauren is glad they will be near grandparents and cousins. "I want to give my kids the opportunity to say, 'I can feel at home in the UK.'"

The education specialists Lauren consulted told her the best time for children to begin boarding school is between the sixth and eighth grade, before they hit their teen years.

"We tend to be planners," explains Lauren. "We started talking with them about it when they were eight or nine, and gave it six months of discussion before deciding. We gave our daughter information on the advantages and disadvantages, but we knew she had to make the final decision. If she didn't want to go, we would plan to stay here until she was twelve and then return to the UK as a family. We told our second daughter the same thing.

"Leah adapted extremely well. We couldn't have asked for anything better. Ellen, our second daughter, has had some struggles. She's more of a 'third culture kid,' less British than Leah, so she has had a harder time adapting. I was always wondering, 'Oh no, what will she say on the phone or in her next e-mail?' They e-mail weekly, and phone every three weeks."

Opportunities

Some people feel they could never send their kids away to school. It's certainly hard to think about when your kids are five or six. "You do hear stories," says Lauren. "I met one British man who went to boarding school when he was seven and didn't see his parents for fifteen years. He said it didn't affect him, but I can't imagine that! As long as my kids are happy and getting input and experience in life, though, even if it's not with me, then I'm happy."

Parenting ❀

Indeed, many of the schooling options available to missionaries may not be able to provide the activities and experiences parents want to give their children. "School is not just math and English. As Europeans, we value extracurricular experience," says Lauren. One woman in her agency whom Lauren admires learned discipline and confidence through her involvement in sports. Lauren wants her daughters to have the same opportunities. "Leah is interested now in cooking. She's learning cake design and design in general, making things out of wood and metal. She also does sports: lifting weights, playing squash, rock climbing. That kind of training provides experience for life."

Maintaining a Healthy Family

Lauren is concerned that her daughters' self-understanding and emotional development might be "flattened" by boarding school, but she is trying to help them from a distance. "If my daughter disagrees with her housemother, she can't discuss it with her like she would with me. I'm trying to get the girls to send us an emotional diary, to make sure they are thinking and talking about their feelings with their friends and with us when they are here."

As Lauren has learned more about parenting and development, she wants to pass her knowledge on to her kids. "Our kids have had lots of Christian input; the girls know their Bibles well and get top marks. But we need to help our kids understand how they tick and how to express their emotions, too. I've learned a lot in the last few years. John Powell's books are brilliant. He wrote *Why Am I Afraid to Tell You Who I Am?* I am going to do a course on that for the teens here, to help them with self-understanding and communication."

Lauren's girls come home three times a year; like many boarding schools, theirs is set up to allow longer breaks with family, including a month at Christmas, a month at Easter, and two months in the summer. "When they aren't here, I have to save up the stuff I want to talk to them about. I want to put new things into practice, but I can't because they aren't here. I concentrate all my parenting into those months. It's too much for Ellen, sometimes!" she says.

In addition to saving up her parenting, Lauren arranges her schedule to allow plenty of family time when the girls are in town. "When they are gone, I do everything I can so that I can be 100 percent free when they are with us. We still have guests, but not as much. At Christmas, we're rather frantic with shopping, socializing, and birthdays; after their friends here go back to school it gets quiet. Their summer visits are less stressful, but I look forward to not living in these cycles!"

Sometimes Lauren feels sorry for Matthew, their youngest and only boy, who is still at home. On the other hand, it's nice for him to be able to do more "boy things" with his sisters out of the picture. He also gets more attention from both parents. "He and his father do Boy Scouts. I can help him with schoolwork. Matthew is our easiest child. It's quite nice to have time with him. I don't feel so stressed with just him. Weekends are quiet."

Now, as Matthew reaches the age at which his sisters went away to school, the family is planning to go back to the UK for a season. They can't afford to have three kids in boarding school, and it would add to their increasing sense of being torn between two continents. Their ministry commitment is coming to an end, and it's been a dozen years since Lauren's husband has worked in his original career field. It will be good for their family to be together for an extended period of time. They have never lived as a family in the UK, since they began work in Central Asia when Leah was just a one year old. Living with their parents again and just going to school during the day may be an adjustment for the girls after several years apart, though: "In boarding school, they have had a lot of independence!"

In the meantime, how does Lauren cope with that feeling of being divided? "It's about letting go. I pray more for my kids than I did before. They are away, not in my control. What can I do? I've learned a lot more about trusting God. He'll look after them."

52 The Right School for Your Kids

"For our kids' education we put them in the British school," says Connie,* an American missionary. "Our reason was that it was medium cost and status—higher status and cost than local schools, but not as high as going to the rich American school," she explains. She and her husband lived and worked in South Asia at the time. "What we never considered was that it put us in another culture. Here we were Americans living in a Muslim culture, trying to break into a minority group within a displaced population, and we had put our kids in a British school. It was very schizophrenic. Our kids didn't know who they were."

Like many frontier workers, Connie and her family had multiple options to choose from for their kids' education, although none of them seemed ideal. "Either the local school or the American school would have been better than what we chose," Connie admits. But how could she have known? There were few places she could turn for good models. Now, some years later, she serves in a position of leadership in her mission agency, and the world has changed. Many people are asking the questions she had then, and sometimes they are asking her. She has many opportunities to help families make decisions about their kids' schooling.

As Connie discovered, every child has different needs at different times in his or her life. Changing plans with their kids' changing needs is something Connie encourages. "As parents we think that if they stick with it, things will get better. We're afraid that if we move them to a new situation, they will lose out."

As her children and their needs changed, Connie's family

---

* For more about Connie, see chapter 3. Loneliness and Adjustment and 33. Choosing Where to Live.

was able to try other models. One child went to a small MK school, and later, to a year of boarding school; the other entered an international school that opened in their city. Others in their organization have sent their children to boarding schools in other countries, while many homeschool or combine homeschooling with local school. There are many good options.

God Works in Your Kids' Lives, Too

Many who come to the field would say their greatest worry is that their kids will not do well. This is a legitimate fear, says Connie. The only problem is the kids will pick up on your concern. "When we first came, worrying about the kids really brought us down, my husband especially," says Connie. "But if the kids think there is something wrong and believe they have a bad life—if you are always trying to compensate and make it up to them, because that's what you believe—they will believe it too. If you praise God for the chance to be overseas and believe it's the best thing for you to be doing—and your kids as well—then they will pick up on that instead."

Now their kids have grown up and are living relatively well-adjusted lives in their home culture, while Connie and her husband are once again overseas. Always a mother, Connie still has fears and worries, but her children's support is a source of strength and peace. "Our daughter wrote an essay to get into college. She was supposed to write about a significant event in her life. She gave it to me to read, and I had tears in my eyes. She wrote about how much she admires her dad and me. She said the four years we were overseas together were the most important years of her life. She said she's a different person because of it, and that she would never want to give that up.

"We tend not to believe hard times are good for our kids. We want to protect them and give them easy lives. But 'easy' is not the only way God works. You have to believe God is working in your kids' lives too, just like he's working in yours."

Parenting

53   One-Room Schoolhouse

Across the courtyard from Trent and Vivian's "main house," five and sometimes six American kids can be found each afternoon, supplementing their local education at Miss Isabelle's English School.[1] They leave their shoes on the steps and enter the brightly decorated room. Two of the ten-year-old students start a fire in the stove or plug in the electric heater. Isabelle's desk looks like any other teacher's desk, and many of the books she uses could be found in a classroom back home in America, but these kids have never attended school in their home country. They and their parents are part of a church-planting team in Central Asia.

And Isabelle? She's the "team teacher." Had she not come, the children's mothers would carry the heavy burden of homeschooling. Many moms do. But a constant flow of neighbors, local believers, and other guests make it nearly impossible for these two mothers to give their kids the kind of attention homeschooling requires. In addition, discipling the women leaders is a crucial part of their team's ministry as church planters and requires of the team women a commitment to language and culture learning. That takes time and energy.

"So rather than taking two women out of action," a teammate explains, "we've gained the services of a third woman!" Isabelle is a full member of the church-planting team and, thanks to her service, so are Vivian and Catherine,* the children's mothers.

---

* For more about Vivian, see chapter 1. Pajamas in Perspective, 7. Why Moms Should Learn the Language, 15. Bringing the Gospel of Peace, 20. Jesus in the Hospital Ward, 23. Available in the Busiest Season, and 42. Even a Healthy Marriage . . . . For more about Catherine, see chapter 26. Sickness, 37. An Answer to My Prayers, 39. Help with House Help, and 47. Helping Your Kids Feel Heard.

Considering the Alternatives

Sending their young children to an international or "missionary" school is not an attractive option for Vivian and Catherine, who do not live near a city with those kinds of schools. With today's technology, education by extension might seem like another option. Like many parts of the developing world, however, Central Asia lacks the reliable phone service and high-speed Internet connections to facilitate this.

"When we came, I was expecting to homeschool them myself," says Catherine, mother of three. "I thought I'd set aside a little classroom area, and that it would just take a couple of hours a day. But that's not how life is, here. Unless I locked the door (which sometimes works!) we were just too interrupted. As a mom, I couldn't be there as much for my kids as a teacher can: I have to answer the door and am distracted thinking about putting my laundry out on the line or having to start dinner. That's what the kids said when Karen, our first team teacher, came. 'She doesn't get up and answer the door every five minutes! She's there with us!'"

Struggling to find someone to take on this role, the team did not expect more than a one-year commitment, but they wanted that year to provide good exposure to cross-cultural ministry for whoever came. They were also wary of taking someone on who would be a burden to them and not connect with the local community. "As we got further into the work, we realized we needed someone who would have a real vision for our ministry and an interest in and love for the people we are working with. Both Karen and Isabelle have really bonded with the people and lived with local families. That has made things so much smoother!" says Vivian.

How It Works

Catherine and Vivian's kids are not solely homeschooled. Six mornings a week the older ones attend local school, while the two youngest attend the equivalent of kindergarten. Going to the neighborhood school with their neighbors helps them live well-adjusted lives in their host country, while Isabelle's "English School" helps them keep up with kids their own age in their home country and ensures they will be ready for college when the time comes. Popular homeschooling resources ease preparation and planning for English School, which requires fifteen to twenty hours a week in the classroom. Isabelle has the rest of her time free for team and ministry activities and keeping up on her own language learning.

Catherine, who serves as the principal of the one-room school, says placing limits on how much time and energy Isabelle gives to teaching has been essential to this immersion process. Planning and grading time are kept to a minimum. When the kids have time off local school, English School usually closes down as well, so Isabelle can have a break. She is also given the freedom to participate in all team events and is included in decision-making.

Now in her second year, Isabelle has begun ministry in the local language as well. She meets weekly with a local believer for Bible study and seeks other opportunities to reach out to friends and neighbors.

"The most successful models I've personally observed," writes a Christian worker from another field, "were the tutors who stayed long enough to become part of the ministry themselves. A short-termer who comes to 'help' can actually 'hinder' if they burden the family with dependence—if they don't know the language, can't get along independently, always need consideration and transportation, and depend on the family for all their social needs."

Catherine and Vivian agree on certain traits that have made Isabelle happy and effective in her role as team teacher.

1. A liking for kids. You do not need professional training for this kind of position any more than the moms who homeschool elsewhere do. However, an aptitude to work well with kids is essential. So are the abilities to work independently and be flexible. "With kids at all levels, I have to switch gears quickly and live with interruptions," explains Isabelle.

2. Sharing the vision. Isabelle shares her team's commitment to church planting, and her desire to bond with the local culture has helped her put down roots in the city. "I don't know much about others who have done this kind of thing, but I imagine it would be hard if you lived with westerners in a protected environment," says Isabelle. "If you don't learn the language, you will only have foreign friends."

3. Ability to do well in an intimate setting. The atmosphere is also more informal than schools back home, something Isabelle sees as a benefit. "The kids like to give massages: I have all these little fists beating on my back while I read them history!" she says. "Sometimes the kids take turns coming to spend the night at my house. They see me as a friend, not the kind of teacher you would be embarrassed to run into at the grocery store."

In addition, Isabelle has enjoyed close relationships with the parents, who are also her teammates and friends. The parents, not Isabelle, set the direction and many of the policies of the small school: Isabelle has to honor and respond to their wishes in their children's education.

4. A vital relationship with God. Both Karen and Isabelle have expected difficulties and have not been chased home by them. When they hit rough places, they go to God for perspective and work through it, with the help of supportive teammates. Their willingness to lay down their careers and identities, as their teammates have done, has been blessed by God.

Discussion Questions for Part 6

Chapter 45: In This as a Family

1. State your philosophy about what it means to do things as a family.

2. How do you include your children in decision-making and help them adjust to upcoming transitions?

3. How does your family's interaction change under stress? What things help you support and understand one another?

Chapter 46: On and Off the Field with Babies

1. With what aspect of Gwen's experience can you identify?

2. Share what effects moving or furloughs have on children. What can you expect? What things can you do to help them?

3. How much do you think a woman with such young children can be involved in outreach ministry?

Chapter 47: Helping Your Kids Feel Heard

1. What are some ways you can help your kids feel heard and valued? What are some of the obstacles?

2. Are there ways you can discipline your children that will make sense to your local friends?

3. How might you include your children in ministry and hospitality?

Chapter 48: Can My Kids Learn This Language?

1. Share your own experiences with the local school or childcare system. What have you heard from others?

2. Donna says language learning is one of the most important things her children need to feel comfortable in their own home. Do you agree? Are there other things that might help children

prosper in a home where their parents entertain guests who speak a different language?

Chapter 49: Finding a Ministry through Parenting

1. How much do you know about your host culture's parenting values and practices? What are some things you like, and what are some things you don't like?

2. How do other foreign women in your host culture respond to local parenting styles? Who could help you understand and respond to the things that are different from your own approach?

Chapter 50: The Perils of Parenting Preschoolers

1. With what aspects of Jennifer's story do you identify? What things might you do the same? What things might you see differently?

2. How do you feel about homeschooling your children? Has God changed your heart or convictions through experiences you have had?

3. What does it mean for you to put family first? Compare and contrast your own needs and practices with Robert and Jennifer's date night and family night.

Chapter 51: Parenting Long Distance

1. Would boarding school be a good option for your children? What stories have you heard about other people's experiences?

2. What would it be like for you to parent "long distance" like Lauren does?

3. Discuss Lauren's comments about helping her children develop emotionally.

Chapter 52: The Right School for Your Kids

1. How are the needs of each of your children different from one another's? Have they changed from year to year?

2. Discuss Connie's assertion that feeling sorry for your kids or trying too hard to protect them can hurt them in the long run.

3. What schooling resources and options are available in your situation? How would you evaluate them?

Chapter 53: One-Room Schoolhouse

1. Can you picture bringing a homeschool teacher to work with your team? What might be the obstacles or costs of this approach?

2. What benefits might a homeschool teacher bring to your team? Do you know someone you might invite to take this role, or would your mission agency be able to help you find someone?

Notes

Introduction

[1] Ruth Tucker, *From Jerusalem to Irian Jaya* (Grand Rapids, MI: Zondervan, 2004), 232.
[2] Frontiers, www.frontiers.org.
[3] Tucker, *Jerusalem*, 233.
[4] Fran Love and Jeleta Eckheart (Pasadena, CA: William Carey Library, 2000).
[5] Mary Ann Cate and Karol Downey (Pasadena, CA: William Carey Library, 2002).
[6] (Grand Rapids, MI: Monarch Books, 2004).

Chapter 7

[1] Trent and Vivian's approach has been documented in their book *Pioneer Church Planting: A Rookie Team Leader's Handbook* (Littleton, CO: Caleb Project, 2001).

Chapter 53

[1] This material has also been published as an article in the homeschooling journal *Interact*.

Other books available from
Authentic Media . . .

Authentic
MEDIA

129 Mobilization Drive
Waynesboro, GA 30830

For a complete catalog of Authentic publications,
please call:

1-8MORE-BOOKS
ordersusa@stl.org

True Grit
Women Taking on the World, for Christ's Sake

Deborah Meroff

Meroff tells the inspiring true adventures of nine 'ordinary' women, both married and single, who are making a difference in such places as Tajikistan, India, Egypt, and Lebanon. We hear about Kathryn, a deaf American who built a ministry to the deaf in Israel; Tammy, who set up businesses in Nepal to help abused women and had to overcome difficulties such as the loss of her visa and former employees setting up a rival business; Pam, who lived and worked in war-racked Tajikistan, a country completely alien and unknown to Westerners; and Cindy, who ended up returning as a missionary to Vietnam after escaping from there as a teenager.

1-850785-75-9

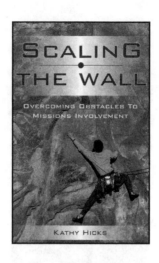

Scaling The Wall
Overcoming Obstacles To Missions Involvement

Kathy Hicks

What is keeping more people from becoming involved in the great commission?

At the Urbana 2001 Missions conference hundreds of college students were posed this question. Their fears were written on a large wall and later collected, compiled and categorized. Fears such as loss of friends, loss of money, disapproval of parents, and inadequate experience surfaced as common obstacles to be overcome.

Missionaries, from many organizations and from around the world who have experienced these same fears, share their personal stories of how God overcame and met their needs in ways they could have never expected.

This book will be helpful to anyone who has fears or reservations about pursuing a role in the world of missions whether short-term, mid-term or life-long.

1-884543-77-4